TEACHING TI LITERACY HOUR
IN AN
INCLUSIVE CLASSROOM

Supporting Pupils with Learning Difficulties in
a Mainstream Environment

1

EDITED BY

ANN BERGER AND JEAN GROSS

David Fulton Publishers Ltd,
Ormond House, 26–27 Boswell Street, London WC1N 3JD

First published in Great Britain by David Fulton Publishers 1999

The rights of Ann Berger and Jean Gross to be identified as the editors of this work have been asserted by them in accordance with the Copyright, Designs and Patents Act 1988.

Copyright © David Fulton Publishers 1999

British Library Cataloguing in Publication Data
A catalogue record for this book is available from the British Library

ISBN 1–85346–630–1

Typeset by FSH Print & P...
Printed in Great Britain by...

Contents

Contributors   iv

Introduction   v
Ann Berger and Jean Gross

Section 1   Including pupils with special educational needs in the Literacy Hour

1   Special needs and the Literacy Hour: some general principles   2
Jean Gross, Ann Berger and Julia Garnett

2   Differentiation in the group work and independent work time   13
Julia Timlin

3   Structured programmes in the Literacy Hour   19
Jean Gross

4   Developing your own structured programme   23
Margaret Hunt and Jennie George

5   Older children working at earlier levels   30
Margaret Hunt and Jennie George

6   Managing behaviour difficulties   34
Jean Gross, Sue Jackson and Jocelyn Atcliffe

Section 2   Two case studies

7   Differentiated planning for a Year 3 class   46
Chris Waldron

8   A class of pupils with global learning difficulties   53
Margaret Tanner

Section 3   Specialist advice on lower incidence needs

9   Children with speech and language difficulties   70
Yvonne Wren

10   Children with hearing losses   78
Sue Young, Helen Walter, Peter Fudge, Ros Way and Ann Berger

11   Pupils with vision impairment   81
Sue Rogers and Joao Roe

12   Children with autistic spectrum disorder   87
Frances Brook and Heather Clewley

Section 4   Using Information and Communication Technology in the Literacy Hour

13   Using Information and Communication Technology   92
Linda Johnson and Ayleen Driver

Index   105

Contributors

Jocelyn Atcliffe	EBD Support teacher
Ann Berger	LEA Adviser
Frances Brook	Support teacher for autistic spectrum disorder
Heather Clewley	Support teacher for autistic spectrum disorder
Ayleen Driver	Curriculum support teacher for ICT
Peter Fudge	Head of Sensory Impaired Children's Service
Julia Garnett	Literacy consultant
Jenny George	Team Leader, Learning Difficulties support team
Jean Gross	Principal Educational Psychologist
Margaret Hunt	Team Leader, Learning Difficulties support team
Sue Jackson	Team Leader, EBD support team
Linda Johnson	Curriculum support teacher for ICT
Joao Roe	Team Leader, Sensory Impaired Children's Service
Sue Rogers	Team Leader, Sensory Impaired Children's Service
Margaret Tanner	Teacher at Florence Brown School
Julia Timlin	Literacy consultant
Chris Waldron	Teacher at Tyning Hengrove Primary School
Helen Walter	Teacher at Henbury Court Primary School
Ros Way	Headteacher, Elmfield School for Deaf Children
Yvonne Wren	Speech and language therapist
Sue Young	Support teacher for hearing impaired children

Introduction

Ann Berger and Jean Gross

Bristol has now been part of the National Literacy Project for over two years. We have learnt about what works within the Literacy Hour for pupils with special needs and have issued guidance to our schools. This book contains much of that guidance.

Each section has been written by a specialist in the field; either an LEA advisory teacher or a teacher from a Bristol school. They are all currently involved in implementing the literacy hour in Bristol schools.

The guidance we have given schools is based on well-tried and tested practice and builds on much of the good work that has taken place in our classrooms. We have tried to help schools to decide how to incorporate the best available techniques and strategies into the literacy hour. The National Literacy Strategy provides a coherent framework and structure, which can benefit pupils of all abilities. Pupils with special needs should be included within this major national initiative. For this to be possible their needs should be planned for carefully. This book is designed to help with this planning and teaching.

Section 1 contains general help and advice about how to organise and plan for pupils' learning within the hour. The section addresses the needs of the majority of pupils with learning difficulties.

Section 2 consists of case studies from two individual teachers who have developed activities which have improved literacy within their classes. The classes include pupils with MLD and EBD.

Section 3 provides specific guidance for teachers who have pupils with less frequent difficulties including visual impairment, hearing impairment, autism, and speech and language disorders.

Section 4 Most pupils with special educational needs (SEN) benefit from the use of information and communication technology (ICT) in order to enhance their skills and access classroom activities. We have included a programme of work which links ICT activities to the learning objectives in the National Literacy Framework, and recommendations for certain software for pupils with special educational needs.

Section 1

Including pupils with special educational needs in the Literacy Hour

1 Special needs and the Literacy Hour: some general principles

Jean Gross, Ann Berger and Julia Garnett

This chapter sets out some general principles for approaching special educational needs within the National Literacy Strategy Framework, and seeks to answer some of the questions teachers and Special Educational Needs Coordinators most often ask about the Literacy Hour.

Introduction

The literacy hour and the National Literacy Strategy Framework have from the beginning been proclaimed as 'for all'. Schools know that they are expected to include all children in the hour, but many have been thrown into confusion by misapprehensions about what this actually means. Others have wondered whether they have to abandon tried and tested support programmes for children with literacy difficulties, because they do not at first sight appear to fit into the new framework.

This book aims to address some of these concerns, and put straight some common misconceptions about the Literacy Hour. It will show how the framework of the hour can accommodate the needs of a wide range of learners, and give practical examples of how this can be done.

The examples, and the guidance, are based on the experience of one local education authority, which was amongst the first cohort to pilot the new national framework, and where the overwhelming feedback from teachers has been that - given hard work and careful planning on their part - children with SEN *have benefited immensely from the introduction of the Literacy Hour, generally find it motivating and helpful, and are making better progress as a result.*

The benefits of the Literacy Hour

Why have these children benefited? One reason is that the Literacy Hour provides a vehicle for quality teaching of literacy, with high knowledge levels on the part of the teacher about what it takes to become literate, and high expectations of what pupils can achieve. Other reasons include the element of structure and predictability of the hour, which is helpful to many pupils, and the regularity of the hour with its daily short bursts of focused teaching followed by practice and reinforcement.

The main reason for the success of the hour with children who have SEN, however, is to be found in the structure of the hour itself. As the National Literacy Strategy framework for teaching additional guidance puts it: 'The structure of the Literacy Hour allows for class teaching that meets individual needs and provides for differentiated group and independent work.' The pattern of shared work, followed by work *matched to the needs of different groups*, and concluded by a motivating plenary when children have the chance to show what they have done and learn from one another, allows the teacher to plan for a wide range of ability.

Elements of the Literacy Hour

The **shared text work** (the first 15 minutes of the hour) has many benefits for children with SEN, because they learn a great deal from the shared experience of texts being read and written by the teacher at a level above that which they can manage independently. Repetition, focused teaching and the support of other learners can provide less confident children with positive and enjoyable experiences of reading and writing as part of the community of literacy learners. Skilful questioning and commenting by the teacher can direct children's attention to aspects of the text appropriate to their particular level and learning needs: class teaching can operate at many levels, and we will provide some examples of how this can be done later in this chapter.

The next section of the hour, **word or sentence level work** (the second 15 minutes) often involves a multi-sensory approach to the teaching of phonics for reading and spelling to the class, where children see and hear how words are made up, blended and segmented. This is particularly helpful to many children with special needs, who will also require a good deal of consolidation and reinforcement – planned for in the small group/independent activity time.

This **small group/independent time** is the part of the hour when this consolidation and reinforcement can be achieved through the kind of structured, systematic programmes which have been used to good effect in the past with children who have SEN. When the Literacy Hour was first introduced, there were widespread misconceptions that this part of the hour had to link directly with the shared text and the shared word and sentence level work in all cases and every day. Teachers feared that this might mean that some children were always working on objectives which were too far advanced (or not advanced enough) for them.

In working with the hour, however, it has become clearer that whilst the skilled teacher can plan differentiated activities following on from the shared text of the week and whole-class work, and will need to do this for some of the time, there must *also* be times when groups of children or individuals can do work which does not link to the shared class work, but addresses basic skills as detailed in children's Individual Education Plans, for example. This work may follow on from the guided reading they do once a week in a group, on books closely matched to their 'instructional' level – the kind of follow up activities, games and worksheets which accompany many reading schemes designed to provide a second chance for struggling readers. Or the work may alternatively take the form of a structured programme designed, for example, to reinforce basic phonic skills.

The final part of the hour, the **plenary**, gives children opportunities for speaking and listening related to their independent work. The teacher can correct misunderstandings, consolidate, revise or extend learning, according to the needs demonstrated in this session. The plenary is also a valuable time for assessing learning, with consequent benefits for children with SEN.

But how do we do it?

Extolling the benefits of the Literacy Hour structure for addressing SEN is one thing. Actually 'doing it', making it work, is another. On the next few pages you will find a collection of some of the concerns and questions which teachers have raised about the practical implementation issues, and some of the answers which we have been able to come up with.

Questions teachers ask about SEN and The Literacy Hour

Do all children in the class have to work on the same text during the Literacy Hour? Or can groups work on reading schemes or structured catch-up programmes during the guided reading and independent activity part of the hour?

Independent activities in the group time do not have to link with the shared text. Groups can work on specific reading schemes or programmes which meet their needs. A theme for the week can be helpful, however, with work for children with weaker literacy skills linked to this shared class time. All children should have at least one task linked to the week's main teaching focus.

What sort of SEN work fits best within the Literacy Hour?

Any ready-made literacy programme which an individual child or a group can do for twenty minutes a day, during the independent/group work of the Literacy Hour – or differentiated work at word, sentence or text level based around the shared text.

What sort of SEN work will not fit into the Literacy Hour framework?

Any programme that takes more than twenty minutes a day will not fit into the Literacy Hour framework. Examples might be Reading Recovery (which involves thirty minutes a day one-to-one withdrawal work) or Family Literacy (where children and parents need an extended period to work together). Some programmes can be partly done in the Literacy Hour and partly outside it – like Oxfordshire's Catch-Up, which needs fifteen minutes one-to-one work each week as well as group work the Literacy Hour.

Should this withdrawal help be arranged during the Literacy Hour framework?

Children should not usually be withdrawn from the Literacy Hour as those with SEN can learn a great deal from the whole session. The Literacy Hour provides most of the child's national curriculum English work; It would not be appropriate to miss out all the time on this essential class learning. Schools will be expected to teach the Literacy Hour to all pupils. This will be inspected by OFSTED. If children are withdrawn their EP needs to specify that this is going to happen, in order to fulfil a particular identified purpose.

So if a child needs extra help – like reading individually to a volunteer, or doing paired reading with an older child – how do we fit this in?

Just like you always have! Children's literacy needs can be addressed outside the Literacy Hour as well as in. Some children will always need extra opportunities to consolidate their learning.

What do we do about children who need an intensive daily dose of word level work (phonics) in Key Stage 2? The Literacy Hour framework doesn't allow for this.

It can be helpful for a child or group to spend a short, focused period (one or two terms) on this type of work, and teachers should not be concerned about planning this if the child really needs it and it does not go on for too long. Care needs to be taken to ensure they have opportunities for extended writing during this period.

What help will children with literacy difficulties need during the Literacy Hour?

You can usefully target Learning Support Assistant time on following a structured daily twenty minute literacy programme with a group of children with SEN. But it is also important to plan some Literacy Hour activities so that children with literacy difficulties can do them without needing extra adult help all the time, just as you did in your teaching before the Literacy Hour was introduced. Activities not involving writing – such as sequencing pictures or sentences, playing a game, or recording through drawings – are the key to this kind of differentiation.

What about setting?

Many schools are setting by literacy ability, especially towards the end of Key Stage 2. This can help you plan lessons where everyone in the room can follow similar work around the shared text. But remember you will still need different activities for pupils who need to work at different levels, even when setting takes place. Remember too that you should plan sets according to the learning difficulties that are appropriate to the individual, not assume that all children with SEN will necessarily be in lower sets. Dyslexic children really benefit from shared text work and plenaries matched to the level of their oral (rather than written) skills. Similarly, a visually impaired child or a child with EBD might need a higher set or a lower set, depending on their individual needs.

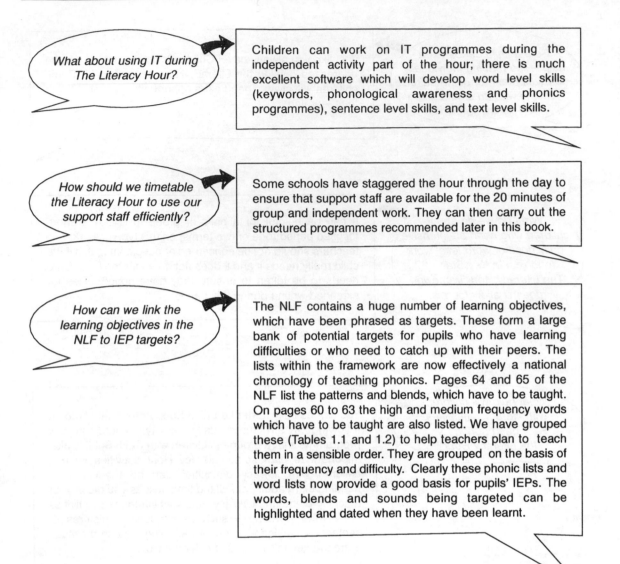

What about using IT during The Literacy Hour?

Children can work on IT programmes during the independent activity part of the hour; there is much excellent software which will develop word level skills (keywords, phonological awareness and phonics programmes), sentence level skills, and text level skills.

How should we timetable the Literacy Hour to use our support staff efficiently?

Some schools have staggered the hour through the day to ensure that support staff are available for the 20 minutes of group and independent work. They can then carry out the structured programmes recommended later in this book.

How can we link the learning objectives in the NLF to IEP targets?

The NLF contains a huge number of learning objectives, which have been phrased as targets. These form a large bank of potential targets for pupils who have learning difficulties or who need to catch up with their peers. The lists within the framework are now effectively a national chronology of teaching phonics. Pages 64 and 65 of the NLF list the patterns and blends, which have to be taught. On pages 60 to 63 the high and medium frequency words which have to be taught are also listed. We have grouped these (Tables 1.1 and 1.2) to help teachers plan to teach them in a sensible order. They are grouped on the basis of their frequency and difficulty. Clearly these phonic lists and word lists now provide a good basis for pupils' IEPs. The words, blends and sounds being targeted can be highlighted and dated when they have been learnt.

Table 1.1 High frequency words grouped by frequency and difficulty

List A	List B	List C	List D
I	we	up	going
and	on	look	away
he	at	like	play
is	for	go	am
a	said	this	cat
to	you	come	day
the	are	big	dog
in	they	my	mum
was	all	no	dad
of		get	yes
it		went	
		me	
		she	
		see	
		can	

These are the first 45 words in the Literacy Framework. We have ordered them according to frequency and difficulty. We suggest you might want to teach them in order – List A then List B etc.

Table 1.2 List 2. The next 154 Literacy Framework words order of frequency and difficulty

List A		List B		List C	
as	that	back	some	about	
be	then	been	their	again	
but	want	by	them	another	
had	when	call(ed)	there	because	pa
have	where	can't	were	brother	saw
him	will	could	what	don't	school
his	an	do	your	door	seen
not	over	first	ball	half	should
one	make	from	bed	help	sister
so	has	her	jump	home	take
with	or	here	got	how	these
little	if	just	than	last	three
down	did	made	man	laugh	time
old	two	more	ran	live(d)	too
new	came	much	good	love	took
		now	girl	many	tree
		off	us	may	very
		our	dig	name	water
		out	house	next	way
				night	would
				once	

Who does what?

Making the Literacy Hour work for children with SEN requires a team approach. The Special Educational Needs Coordinator (SENCO), class teacher and a range of additional adults who may be working in the classroom (Learning Support Assistants or parent helpers, for example) all have different but vital roles to play.

The role of the SENCO

The role of the SENCO will be to:

- advise colleagues on how to differentiate their teaching during the Literacy Hour so as to meet the needs of a wide range of learners;
- organise support staff to work in the Literacy Hour as effectively as possible with small groups of children, pairs or individuals;
- coordinate IEPs so that they take account of the literacy framework and link with what will happen to the child during the Literacy Hour.

The role of the support teacher

Some schools are lucky enough to have support teachers to provide skilled help for children with SEN. Such teachers can work in a variety of ways, for example:

- with a group/groups during independent activity time either in or out of the classroom;
- preparation or follow-up work related to the current shared text for the class;

after the shared session with the whole class, working with the SEN group on word
work at their level;
- taking a group for a literacy hour of their own;
- outside the Literacy Hour on short-term intensive interventions such as a 'catch up'
programme.

The role of the LSA or parent helper

A larger group of schools will be able to deploy at least some additional support from
Learning Support Assistants or parent helpers. Such additional adults can be involved
in:

- Supporting in shared text time by:
    - sitting with children who are easily distracted to direct and focus attention
    - sharing a copy of the same text with an individual child, in the group on the
    carpet or at a desk near the group, running a pointer or finger under the text as
    the teacher reads
    - reading the same text with a small group, i.e. parallel session in the room
    - monitoring specific children's behaviour/attention/concentration/ responses
    for the teacher.

- Supporting in word/sentence level time by
    - monitoring individual children's responses, e.g. spelling, letter formation,
    reading of words when asked.

- Supporting in group activity time by:

    - working with one or two groups on differentiated tasks arising from the shared
    or guided sessions with the teacher, to consolidate key points
    - working with one or two groups to prepare them for forthcoming work, e.g. the
    next day's shared text
    - working with one or two groups on structured activities planned by the teacher
    or SENCO, e.g. phonological awareness programmes such as 'Sound
    Beginnings', 'Sound Works'; reading scheme activities such as Wellington
    Square, fuzzbuzz, etc
    - working with individual pupils: on their IEP, on differentiated group tasks,
    listening to them read, supporting their writing.

- Supporting in the plenary by

    - monitoring individuals' responses
    - helping children to feed back.

- Supporting outside the Literacy Hour

    - this should relate to the teaching objectives for the child/group and could
    comprise preparation or follow-up work around the shared text; listening to
    children reading, monitoring and assessing progress informally.

Finally, teachers should not underestimate the potential role of other children in the team
approach to helping children with SEN to learn. Peer tutoring or partner learning was well
established in many schools before the advent of the Literacy Hour, and can be extremely
effective for both 'tutor' and 'tutee'. There is no reason why older children cannot work
with younger children (for example, on paired reading or over a computer program)
during the Literacy Hour, with a little careful whole-school timetabling and planning.
Again, within one class group certain independent activities can be arranged in mixed

ability groupings (collaborative writing tasks, for example), or in pairings – so as to capitalise on the potential for children to help each other to learn.

How can the class teacher adapt her teaching to meet a range of needs?

In this chapter we have looked at some very general principles about the potential benefits of the Literacy Hour for children with SEN, and at some of the issues of planning and management. Ultimately, however, success will depend on the very specific and practical ways in which class teachers adapt their teaching style so as to include the needs of all children. In the next section you will find some suggestions on the adaptations which can be made. They are based on observed good practice, and can be used as a bank of ideas on which to draw when planning for individual children, or as a self-assessment checklist for all teachers who would like to work towards being more inclusive in their teaching style.

SEEING

❑ Can all the children see your face?

❑ Have you made sure your back is not to the window? Can all the children see the text – is the print size big enough and any photocopying clear?

LISTENING

❑ Have you made the room's acoustics as good as you can, at least by shutting the door?

❑ Have you tried to avoid background noise such as noisy heaters and buzzing lights?

❑ Do you check for understanding – by asking a child who may or may not have got the point, to explain back to you what you have said?

❑ Do you write up new vocabulary as you introduce it (words like 'phoneme') and keep on a chart in the room... return to it to revise and reinforce?

❑ Do you put up a glossary of word meanings for new/difficult vocabulary?

❑ When you ask a child a question do you preface it with his or her name to focus attention?

❑ Do you give the child time to think and answer?

❑ Do you rephrase the question in other words if the child looks lost?

ATTENDING AND BEHAVING

❑ Have all the children got room?

❑ Are you using a developmental progression in seating?

Focus on Big Book	Yr R	All the children on the carpet
	Yr 3	Children on the carpet plus some bean bags, a bench or one row of chairs
	Yr 5	Children on the carpet plus a row of chairs in front of other children sitting at desks
Focus on OHT	Yr 6	Children sitting at desks or in two semi-circles of chairs around the enlarged text or OHT.

❑ Is everyone clear about the Literacy Hour routine – do you have the routine (written and drawn) up on a chart on the wall? Do you point to a clock to show the children where they are in the hour's routine?

❑ Have you put a 'Do Not Disturb' notice on your door?

❑ Do you positively acknowledge individual children for paying attention and sitting still (using for example, a private agreed signal like 'thumbs up' or using words such as 'I like the way John is sitting still and listening hard')?

❑ When one child is writing on a flip chart or board, or making words with magnetic letters, have you made sure they stand to one side while doing this so the rest of the class can see?

❑ Do you keep up a running commentary to keep the other children involved, or give them a role (like something to watch out for)?

❑ Do you clearly tell the children what the objectives are for the week and what they will be learning?

CONTRIBUTING

❑ Do you involve less able children in some way in the text even if it is a difficult one for them e.g. give them a letter or a word written on a card and ask them to watch out for it in the text?

❑ Do you give children with SEN activities in shared reading so that they are fully part of what is going on and don't have to sit still all the time – ask them to open the shared book, turn the pages, show the teacher where to begin reading, hold the pointer or point to the text as the class reads, frame a letter or a word with a masking device, circle a capital letter, draw round a word with a pen on an acetate overlay, hold and read out a prepared question card?

❑ In shared writing do you use the same idea of actively involving children with SEN – asking them to show the teacher where to begin writing or where to leave space, to contribute oral ideas, to go to the writing table and find a word card, to write a high frequency word in the story or write in a full stop?

❑ In word level work, do you try to be lively and use visual/touch stimulus – games, songs, trays of objects, photo cards, plastic letters, thin card strips for alliterative phrases, cloud-shaped card for 'new words we like', brick shaped cards for tricky words, word wheels, chopped up cards to piece together?

❑ In word level work, do you involve children physically and actively in holding cards, circling words and letters, writing on the white board or a mini board of their own, fishing for high frequency word fish from a bowl, attaching the 'new words we like' to the wall display or sticking a letter in order on an alphabetical word snake?

❑ When you ask questions, do you ask open questions for more able pupils, and for less able children more closed questions or questions which give a choice – 'Do you think it's x or do you think it's y?'

❑ When children answer can you 'echo back' what they have said, in expanded and grammatically correct form?

❑ In shared writing, can you take an idea from a less able child and ask a more able child to add to it (That's a lovely idea, Mark... Can you think of some describing words to add to it, John?)?

❑ Could you prepare children with SEN for the shared reading text by having them listen to it on tape beforehand?

GUIDED READING

❑ Are you choosing books carefully so that they are at the children's instructional level? (No more than ten words in a hundred that they can't read).

❑ Are the books appropriate to the childrens' age and dignity - high interest age/low reading age books at KS2?

❑ Do the books you have chosen have back-up activities for independent work – to reinforce the vocabulary etc?

❑ Do you take extra care to prepare the children for the guided read by talking through the book page by page before they start, introducing all new vocabulary this way?

❑ Can you find a way for the children to practice reading the book several times after they have read it in guided reading – to parents (if you have enough sets of the books to let them be taken home), to a more able reading partner in independent work time, or to a younger child?

INDEPENDENT GROUPWORK

❑ Have you spent several weeks (before you start guided reading) teaching your class how to work independently, developing and writing up 'rules', getting them used to the signal (like a red flag on a table) that shows you are busy and not to be approached, using a whole–class reward system (like marbles in a jar leading to a class treat when the jar is full) to reinforce independent working, and building up slowly the time they are asked to work independently?

❑ Do you carry on using a planned reward system for independent working from time to time, even when the children have got used to it, taking care to give extra opportunities to children who find it difficult to be noticed for working well on their own?

❑ Do you praise children for working well independently much more often than you admonish them when they aren't?

❑ Do children have laminated cards saying 'six things to do before asking the teacher...?'

❑ Are you organised? Is everything the children need there for them on each table? Do you have classroom monitors to help get everything ready? Do children know where to put finished work?

❑ Have children practised the routines of moving from activity to activity during the Literacy Hour?

❑ Do you give clear signals when it is time to move from shared time to group work (and then to plenary)? Do you use an LSA to give some children extra practice in going through the routines, and to give them extra praise and reinforcement when they are seen following them?

❑ Do you use a pictorial task board so the children can see what their group is expected to do and when?

❑ Do you put a task card on each table so children can refer to it if they forget what they are meant to do? Have the task cards got visual clues and clear instructions (eg: 'you will need...?')

❑ Are your task cards and worksheets in readable language – short sentences, active not passive verbs, making instructions stand out boldly, making the page well spaced out and uncluttered?

❑ Have you modelled (in the shared word or sentence level work) at least one or two of the tasks so that children will not come to them 'cold'?

❑ Have some children with special needs got a 'circle of friends' you have organised, to whom they can go for help if they get stuck in independent group time?

❑ Have you considered pairing a more able with a less able group in independent group time, so that you can arrange collaborative activities in a mixed ability way and make maximum use of children learning from and helping one another?

❑ Do you have lists of key high frequency words around the classroom or on desk mats?

❑ Are you planning alternatives to paper and pencil tasks – children preparing oral presentations or tape recordings; representing information in pictures/diagrams/flow charts; computer-aided recording; sequencing prepared sentences or filling in missing words in text; using cooperative writing in groups or pairs; using prepared writing frameworks/prompt sheets; clipping letter cards onto pictures with clothes pegs; matching upper case to lower case plastic letters; blu-tacking words under the text of a big book in the correct order or sequencing cut up laminated pages of favourite books?

❑ Have you differentiated the group tasks so that children with SEN can do them without extra adult help, for example by leaving cards with words they will need on their table, by providing them with a pre-prepared structure/ framework to write from, or by using information books with harder and easier versions of the same text?

❑ Do you know about the whole literacy framework, not just 'your' key stage; if you are a KS2 teacher have you had a chance to observe KS1 literacy hours so that you can see at first-hand the things some of your children will still need to be learning and doing?

PLENARY

❑ Are you making maximum use of the plenary to motivate children in their independent groupwork – preparing them by telling them exactly what they will be asked to feed back during the plenary?

❑ Could pairs of children feed back together if they lack confidence?

❑ Can you plan for visual ways of feeding back where children have language difficulties?

❑ Could the children use props – speaking through a puppet, for example?

❑ Can you use 'small steps' – starting with a tiny contribution the child is comfortable with and building up?

❑ Have you created a climate in the class of children giving each other feedback in helpful ways – for example by handing out sentence cards 'I liked the way' or 'a helpful idea for the author would be...', for children to read out after a plenary presentation.

2 Differentiation in the group work and independent work time

Julia Timlin

In this chapter we look at ways in which teachers can plan for differentiation within the Literacy Hour, so as to provide work which is pitched at the right level.

Promoting independence in the group activity part of the hour is not specific to children with special needs. All children need clear ground rules and strategies for working successfully together. Many of these process skills need to be directly taught and reinforced at every opportunity.

The possible types of tasks

The tasks need to address the National Literacy Strategy objectives which have been chosen for that specific block of work. They also need to be addressing the specific needs of the identified group of pupils.

When planning the tasks, consideration needs to be given to the level of reading or writing that is involved and whether this would restrict the independence of some children. For children with specific learning difficulties/ dyslexia this can be particularly important: often these children can conceptually grasp the task but are held back by long written instructions or demands for written responses.

We often recommend that children are taught *how* to do the activity. This might be through instruction, modelling or demonstration. In this way classes can gradually build up a range of activities with which they are familiar and which require minimal explanation and reading of instructions. The best tasks are those where the children are very familiar with the idea and are able to transfer their knowledge of the type of task from week to week even though the content will change. Children will quickly build up a repertoire of familiar generic activities that they enjoy and will learn from.

These 'active learning activities' might include the following.

Reading

- Re-reading familiar books, poems, jokes.
- Reading, sequencing, matching, retelling the big book.
- Responding to a text orally, or through another medium, e.g. art, construction.
- Reading and following instructions.

Writing

- Working on a *part* of the writing process (planning/drafting/revising/redrafting/editing/publishing).
- Developing writing from shared writing.

Active Learning Activities particularly suitable for Key Stage 2 need to provide alternatives to traditional written responses. They can include:

Text Marking

Using either a simplified or alternative piece of text.

Word Level

- Spelling patterns, e.g. highlight all or some of the words
  (a) ending with...(b) beginning with...
- Make a list of the words or make them with plastic letters etc. (these words could be high frequency words or words with the same spelling pattern).

Sentence Level

- Highlighting names, nouns, verbs, adjectives, etc. (this can be done using the big book text of the week, or an appropriate simplified text that matches the genre focus).
- Compiling a list, e.g. ingredients in a recipe.
- Making a poster, e.g. using adjectives that describe a known character from the text.

Text Level

- Fiction
  - words or phrases describing character or setting
  - add the words round a picture of a character or scene
  - colour in picture only if colours are mentioned in description.

- Non-Fiction
  - one or two colour underlining to highlight key information
  - limit number of words to be marked
  - follow by list, pattern or chart (partly completed, e.g. Victorian clothes).

Sorting

- Sort objects
  - that begin/do not begin with the same phoneme
  - that may/may not appear in an extract.

- Sort pictures and words
  - linked with the shared text
  - linked to word/sound knowledge.

- Sort a bank of words into
  - ABC order
  - 1, 2, 3 syllables
  - noun/verb.

Sequencing

- Picture/sentence.
- Words to make the sentence – different colours for different parts, e.g. nouns = red.
- Word order – questions into statements, e.g. Are we going home?, We are going home.
- Lines from poems.
- Pictures from the focus text or guided reading book.
- Paragraphs from the big book or guided reading book.

Coding systems

- Punctuating with counters (second best – sticky dots)
    - using coloured counters as full stops to punctuate sentences in a given extract.
    - using different coloured counters for different punctuation.
- Punctuating with sounds, e.g. musical instruments
    - as above, but using instruments to represent the punctuation marks.

Cloze

- Word Level
    - rhyming couplets (second rhyming word) in poems, e.g.:

        On the Ning Nang Nong
        Cows go B_____!

- Sentence Level
    - missing nouns or verbs, etc. on cards to put into a text.
- Text Level
    - fill in names of characters in simplified description (relate back to the main shared text) e.g._____ has a green coat and a moaning voice
    - whole lines of shared poem, containing a rhyming clue
    - delete labels from diagrams, use words on cards to re-label.

Matching

- Speech in bubble to speech in narrative text – sort and/or fill in 'who said what?' grid.
- Phrases and/or sentences on cards, match to the appropriate character from the shared text (use grid or pictures of characters).

Read and draw/Read and do

- Note making in the form of a picture – draw or complete the picture.
- Use a verse of a shared poem to generate a picture of a character, setting, etc., e.g. The Adventures of Isabel by Ogden Nash, The Owl and the Pussy Cat by Edward Lear.
- Instruction cards – walk around school.

Differentiation of tasks

Matching work to the needs of each ability group, which lasts for the appropriate amount of time and is challenging, is quite a complex task.

Teachers can and have successfully differentiated work for a range of abilities when they have chosen to do a whole-class follow up activity (especially at Key Stage 2). If this is the case, careful consideration needs to be given to the differentiation of that task, its appropriateness for those children with SEN, and how it is meeting the needs (and possibly IEPs) of those children.

Tasks can be differentiated in one or a combination of three ways:

- By adult support – where the task may remain the same for every group, but the adult intervention of careful questioning and 'just the right amount' of support provides the differentiation.
- By input – which needs prior consideration and careful planning by the teacher. Some pupils may need a variety of support mechanisms to be able to complete the task successfully, whist others can complete the same task without any extra support (e.g. using words cards/banks, objects, writing frames, working with a partner or group).
- By outcome – where the learning objective for all pupils is the same, but it will be achieved at a different level by the range within the class. For example, the objective

for a Year 4 class is to 'collect and classify examples of verbs'. The most able group might be searching for and highlighting speech verbs from an unknown text, use a thesaurus to extend their collection which they then use to improve their own independent writing. A middle group may be searching for speech verbs in the big book and listing them on a grid (see Figure 2.1).

Question verbs	Verbs used for a talking voice	Verbs used for a raised voice

Figure 2.1 Grid for listing speech verbs

The least able group might be given a piece of text with the speech verb 'said' used every time. A selection of appropriate verb cards are provided and the pupils have to substitute the 'said' to make the extract more interesting. Figure 2.2 illustrates the range of task differentiation, and relates to term 1 in a Year 3 class. The National Literacy objectives for Week 1 of a two week block on fiction are:

Text Level

- To compare a range of story settings and select words and phrases describing scenes.
- To express views about a story or poem, identifying specific words and phrases to support a viewpoint.
- To develop the use of settings in own stories by writing short descriptions of known places; writing a description in the style of a familiar story.
- To collect suitable words and phrases, in order to write poems and short descriptions; design simple patterns in words; use repetitive phrases; write imaginative comparisons.

Sentence Level

- To use verb tenses with increasing accuracy in speaking and writing, e.g.
  - Catch/caught, see/saw, go/went etc.
  - Use past tense consistently for narration.

Word Level

- To discriminate syllables in reading and spelling (from Year 2).
- To collect new words from reading and work in other subjects and create ways of categorising and logging them.
- To infer the meaning of unknown words from the context.

Group A is identified as the most able and Group E as the children with special needs; Groups B, C, and D are between the two extremes.

On Monday, notice the tasks set for groups A and B. They have been differentiated by outcome, although they also have the support of another adult. The words for the syllable task for groups D and E have been selected to match the focus words to be learnt by the group, i.e. high frequency and words with particular phonemes.

On Wednesday, Groups B, C and D are all given the same task with only C group having other adult support.

Range: stories with familiar settings. Texts: Extract 1 from *The Magicians Nephew* by CS Lewis, extract 2 from *Anneli the Art Hater* by Anne Fine and the poem *Up Inside the Attic* by Richard Edwards.

YEAR 3 TERM 1	Whole class – shared reading and writing	Whole class – word and sentence level work	Group A	Group B	Group C	Group D	Group E	Plenary
MONDAY	Introduce block of work on settings. Read 1st extract from 'every bit'. Ask children which sort of room it is. Find evidence in the text. Reveal from 'it was shaped...' 'What is an attic/sitting room etc.? List the objects in the room.	Revise syllables from Year 2. Use children's names as a starting point. Then with objects and words from the extract...clapping. Go through the sentence 'it was shaped....' counting syllables. Make decision about hyphenated words.	Identify 2 and 3 syllable words in the extract. Highlight in two colours, then put the words on a grid. / OA	Identify 2 and 3 syllable words in the extract. Highlight in two colours, then put the words on a grid if enough time. / OA	Sort word cards into words with 1, 2 and 3 syllables. / I	Sort word cards into words with 1 and 2 syllables, check with a partner (use HF and focus words). / Guided reading T	Guided reading / T / Sort word cards into 1 and 2 syllables, check with a partner (use HF and focus words). / I	Groups A and C feed into plenary. How did you sort the words?
TUESDAY	Remember what was in the attic. Re-read extract 1 listening for detail. Individual children to recall detail about the objects on the list made yesterday. Highlight these on the text. Teacher models redrafting.	Use some of the extract words as a starting point for spelling words with 2 syllables. Sum/mer, ham/mer, num/ber, yel/low, big/ger, at/tic.	Using the poem 'Up inside the attic', generate a list of objects including descriptive phrases. Identify unfamiliar words with a * / I	Guided reading / T	Using the poem 'Up inside the attic', highlight objects in one colour and descriptive phrases in another. / OA	In pairs – highlight the objects on the poem. Circle words that they do not know. / I	Using words from the shared reading list sort the words into two sets. 'In my house' 'Not in my house' Write words on the correct list. / I	Feedback on unfamiliar words with the whole class. / Group E report on their task. / Discuss.
WEDS	Introduce extract 2 – repeat plan as Monday.	Identify misspelt words in specially typed text of 'The Magicians Nephew'. Use segmenting words into syllables to aid spelling.	Guided reading / T	Give children a copy of extract 2. Ask the children to the text to include as much detail as possible. / Group B–I	Group C–I	Group D–OA	Give the children a sheet with Jodies room. Ask children to draw objects they can remember and from the shared reading list. / Group E–OA	Show a selection of drawings, comment on the detail – colour, shape, objects etc. derived from the text. Draw attention to omissions
THURS	Using extract 2 – repeat plan as Tuesday. Have story sack of objects from both extracts and discuss which text extract each object comes from. Refer back to the texts for evidence.	Matching descriptive phrases to nouns. eg, 'silky scarlet' to 'ribbons' Then sort according to text origin	Guided reading / Group A–I	Group B–I	Guided reading / T / Group C–I	Using the objects from the story sacks, work as a group to match the 'phrase' with the objects. Work led by another adult. / Group D–I	Group E–OA	Groups D and E hold up objects and the other groups match with the correct descriptions.
FRIDAY	Introduce a picture of a room. Shared writing, describing the room in the picture using the process used over the week. 1. List objects they can see. 2. Add details. 3. Write description the room. Draw attention to to the importance of using the appropriate tense consistently and writing in full sentences – extend words and phrases generated. Edit questions – full stops, capital letters	Writing descriptions of a room (pictures provided)	Group A–I	Group B Guided writing / Group B–T	Group C–I	Group D–OA	Group E–OA	Focus on consistent use of tense in the children's writing. Choose selection from each group then report back to the class.

Figure 2.2 Differentiation in planning

OA = Other Adult Support   I = Independent   T = Teacher Support

You will be able to see where the task, in some instances, is quite different for some groups: however, the learning intention remains the same, it is only the route to that learning that differs.

Group organisation

The organisation of the groups does not need to be fixed. It may be that the children will need to work in a number of different ways to maximise their learning potential. Pupils might work individually, in pairs, in mixed ability groups and within ability groups. The teacher will be working with a guided reading or writing group (children with similar needs/ability) and this often influences the class organisation in this part of the hour.

Use of other adults

Nearly all children are capable of working independently if the support structures and mechanisms are provided. However, children with SEN benefit from the additional support of working with LSAs or other adults. In the Literacy Hour this can be used in a number of ways.

- Whole-class shared reading and writing, word and sentence level work.

  To support one to one
  - sitting together at a table nearby with a small copy of the big book encouraging responses
  - managing behaviour
  - assessment
  - answering the teacher's questions to stimulate pupil's responses.

- Guided, group and independent activities.

  To support one to one
  - working on specific word or sentence work
  - working on objective related IEP targets
  - individual reading
  - intensive support with the task.

  To support a group
  - with a group task
  - leading group reading
  - reinforcing/developing word level work
  - working towards objective linked group/IEP targets.

- Plenary

  To support one to one or group
  - to feed back
  - assessments.

Conclusion

When using extra support in these ways, we still need to think of how the child can increasingly learn to be less reliant on adults, and increasingly independent. As teachers, this is a crucial part of our work and not a by-product of working uninterrupted elsewhere. With this in mind, teachers need to plan carefully for differentiation strategies, and for ways of developing process skills in the class as a whole. The ideas outlined in this chapter provide a framework in which these issues can be addressed.

3 Structured programmes in the Literacy Hour

Jean Gross

This chapter discusses the use of structured 'catch up' programmes during the Literacy Hour. It recommends particular programmes which are likely to be effective and give good value for money.

Introduction

When the Literacy Hour was first introduced many teachers assumed that *all* children in their class would need to spend the whole of the hour on work related to the shared class text. They were worried about what would happen to their poor readers, and whether they had to throw out the structured programmes and schemes they had been using, often successfully, to help these readers 'catch up' with basic skills.

Experience soon made clear, however, that the Literacy Hour does *not* mean dispensing with all of these well-tried methods. The 20 minutes a day independent and group work can in fact provide an ideal framework for such structured intervention programmes: the very regularity and consistency of this daily pattern allows for the 'little and often' principle which we know works best for children with literacy difficulties.

Any structured intervention programme used in the hour needs, nevertheless, to be clearly focused on particular objectives from the National Literacy Framework. It also needs to be time-limited, with children's progress closely monitored, so that children do not go on with a restricted diet of, for example, word level work only, for any longer than they need to.

This means that we need to make a careful choice in the structured interventions we use, selecting only those which have a proven track record of making a substantial, sustainable difference to children's basic literacy skills, within a relatively short period.

This chapter aims to provide information on some of the structured programmes and schemes which fall into this category. It focuses on those interventions which will fit in with the 20 minutes a day framework of the Literacy Hour. Most of them are about word and sentence level work; most of them are about reading rather than writing. This is why it is important that children working on them still have access to text level work, shared writing and so on through the shared time in the hour, and the plenary.

Some highly effective, thoroughly evaluated structured intervention programmes will *not* fit the 20 minute a day model.

Programmes based on one to one adult support may be better timetabled *outside* the hour: for example, Reading Recovery, which involves 30 minutes a day of one to one teaching, every day, for a period of 8 to 12 weeks. Similarly Family Literacy programmes cannot be accommodated within the Literacy Hour structure; Family Literacy courses run for eight hours a week; each week there are two separate sessions (parents in one room, children in another) and one joint session.

Such programmes are, however, too effective to jettison: many schools are achieving success by building in a Family Literacy programme as well as the Literacy Hour, which takes place at a different time of day, and targets children for whom effective home support is likely to be the key to long-term success, for a short (12 week) focused period.

Some programmes fit the Literacy Hour structure in part, but need additional planned time together for child and teacher outside the hour. Oxfordshire's Catch Up programme is one example. This programme targets Year 3 children who have not attained Level 2 in their end of Key Stage 1 SATs. Each child on the programme has one ten minute session a week of one to one help from the classroom teacher. In addition there is a group reading session lasting 15 minutes once a week. This session can easily be incorporated into the Literacy Hour group time, as long as the teacher is able to arrange the individual sessions for the children outside the hour. Photocopy masters and a CD-ROM of literacy games are available in addition and can be used by children in independent time, to practise basic skills without adult support. The programme lasts a full school year and initial evaluation has been encouraging.

Structured programmes which work well

In this section we will look at programmes aimed at children with reading difficulties which can readily be accommodated within the Literacy Hour – so long as additional adult help (a trained Learning Support Assistant or teacher) is available.

Phonological awareness programmes

Weak phonological awareness is one of the main causes of reading difficulty, and there is considerable research evidence to show that programmes aimed at developing poor readers' phonological awareness in Key Stage 1 have a long-lasting impact on their later reading and spelling ability. One programme which is based on this research is *Sound Beginnings* (LDA). This pack provides structured activities, suitable for a classroom assistant to use with a small group, based on training phonological awareness through oral rhyming and alliteration tasks followed later by tasks using plastic or wooden letters and picture cards. Children can work with an assistant once a week in a group on these activities, and on other days use the worksheets and games from the pack to back up their learning as part of independent work within the hour.

Another phonological awareness programme is *Launch into Reading Success* (Psychological Corporation). This is similarly aimed at young children (Key Stage 1). It provides the outline of a comprehensive series of short sessions, very clearly described and suitable for a classroom assistant or support teacher to do with a group of children over a period of perhaps one to two terms. Its effectiveness has not been formally evaluated, but many teachers are finding it useful.

Phonics programmes

Once children with reading difficulties have acquired basic phonological awareness they will need to work on basic phonic skills through methods which provide higher levels of structure, repetition and reinforcement than may be necessary for the majority of children. Structured phonic programmes abound, and many special needs teachers will have particular favourites which have worked for them in their setting and can be fitted into the Literacy Hour group and independent time without too much difficulty. Below we focus on three particular programmes which have been fairly rigorously evaluated over a number of settings and where teachers can feel reasonably confident in the outcome, if they are used by a trained adult with the regularity and frequency the

Literacy Hour allows. It is important to use different programmes for pupils of different ages to encourage pupils' self-esteem.

DISTAR

DISTAR is a group programme which takes children in Key Stage 1 or 2 with no initial phonic knowledge through initial sounds to C-V-Cs, and words containing blends and digraphs. Lessons are carefully scripted and based on solid principles of what makes for effective learning. Attention is paid to motivation and each piece of new learning carefully builds on the last, with much repetition and opportunity for children to become really fluent in reading words containing each sound. The lessons are meant to be delivered through short, daily group sessions and are thus ideal as a 'catch up' programme within the Literacy Hour.

THRASS

THRASS (Teaching Handwriting, Reading and Spelling Skills) is a structured multi-sensory programme which teaches children about letters, speech sounds and spelling choices. It teaches children the 44 spoken sounds (phonemes) of the English language, and the different ways in which each can be represented in writing. It is suitable for small group work within the Literacy Hour but does require training for the adults involved. Computer software is available so that children can follow up group sessions with independent work. It is particularly suitable for use in Key Stage 2.

Soundworks

This a relatively new multi-sensory phonological awareness and phonics group programme for five to eight year olds. It was specifically designed for use by classroom assistants, parents or other volunteers and fits very well into the 20 minutes a day framework. It begins by teaching children the basic consonant letter sounds and how to distinguish initial and final sounds in words they hear. It goes on to C-V-C words, some digraphs and initial consonant blends. By the end of the course, which takes roughly two terms, children will know the five short vowel sounds, and some suffixes, and will also have tackled a number of high frequency irregular words.

With all these phonic programmes, a useful pattern for the Literacy Hour is to try and have a small group of children work on them three times a week, reserving the other two sessions for guided reading with the teacher, and for a differentiated activity which links in with the class focus for the week and on which the group can report back during the plenary time.

Individual work

As well as the small-group programmes we have described above, the Literacy Hour structure allows children with literacy difficulties to spend time during the small group and independent time on individual or paired activities. Here the research evidence indicates that computer-based programmes – and in particular the use of 'Talking Computers' – are particularly effective.

The 'Talking Computer' programme (also known as the 'Somerset Talking Computer Project', 'Talking Pendown' and the 'Jersey Computer Assisted Reading Development Programme') allows the child to work on finely graded materials consisting of phonically based sentences, which he or she reads, repeats from memory, and types onto a computer. The child immediately 'hears' what he or she has written spoken back, allowing for self-correction.

Evaluation has shown that children are highly motivated by the approach and make rapid gains in reading and spelling skills over even a short period – four weeks of 20 minutes a day individual work with an adult helper.

New developments

Materials have recently been developed by a team of National Literacy Strategy consultants, aimed at providing a 'catch up' programme for groups of Year 3 and 4 children to work on several times a week with a classroom assistant. Funding is available nationally for schools to employ additional assistants to implement the programme, which focuses on word level objectives and is specifically designed to be fully compatible with the National Literacy Framework. As such, the programme is likely to be highly influential and definitely one to watch out for.

Also well worth investigating is Phonographix (also called Reading ReFlex), another highly structured phonic approach which came from the USA and is intended to be delivered by teachers or volunteers who have had intensive training in the methodology. Initial results in schools using the approach in the UK have been very promising.

Using reading schemes

Some publishers have already brought out reading schemes designed for work in the Literacy Hour with children who have literacy difficulties (Ginn's Springboard, Collins' Jumpstart, for example). Many more are likely to follow. They tend to include back-up materials covering all elements of the Literacy Framework – some phonic 'catch-up' work, work on high frequency words, sentence and text level activities. In this sense they may provide the teacher with useful ideas for independent work to follow on from guided reading of books from the scheme – but may not have the same impact as the more structured programmes we have been looking at in this chapter. They do not always break new learning down into small enough steps, or provide enough repetition and multi-sensory reinforcement.

It is not difficult, however, to take the books from these or any other reading scheme already in use in the school, and devise a series of daily group activities which *will* provide a multi-sensory approach with high levels of reinforcement. It is to guidance on this that we turn in the next chapter.

Further information

Catch Up: The Catch Up Project, School of Education, Oxford Brookes University, Wheatley, Oxford OX33 1MX.

DISTAR: Science Research Associates, Mackaw and Hill Publishing Company, Shoppen Hagar, Maidenhead, Berks SL6 2QL.

Family Literacy: Adult Literacy and Basic Skills Unit, PO Box 293, London WC1V 7DW.

Launch into Reading Success: Psychological Corporation, Foots Cray High Street, Sidcup, Kent DA14 5HP.

Reading Recovery: The Reading Recovery National Network, University of London Institute of Education, 20 Bedford Way, London WC1 HOAL.

Sound Beginnings: LDA, Duke Street, Wisbech, Cambs PE13 2AE.

Soundworks: The Open School, Park Road, Totnes, Devon TQ9 6EQ.

Talking Computers: Talking Systems, 22 Heavitree Road, Exeter, Devon EX1 2LQ.

THRASS: Collins Educational.

4 Developing your own structured programme

Margaret Hunt and Jennie George

It is possible that you do not have access to structured programmes described in the previous chapter, but that you do have multiple copies of an existing scheme aimed at struggling readers. What can you do then? It is relatively easy to devise your own five step weekly programme around one text per week, taken from such a reading scheme. This chapter will be particularly useful when planning for pupils with specific learning difficulties and dyslexia as it encourages multi-sensory approaches and overlearning.

Any programme used in the Literacy Hour needs to be based on a recognition that children who struggle to acquire literacy skills need intensive teaching and opportunities to 'overlearn' word level objectives – that is, to practise phonic links and key word recognition well beyond the point where they appear to have mastered them. If they do not have opportunities to do this then they will rapidly forget new learning. They also need to learn using all their senses – seeing words and letters, hearing them, and feeling them: this is called multi-sensory learning.

The five day programme

A five day programme suitable for these children is described below. It is designed to support the needs of children requiring a 'daily dose' of basic literacy strategies. It can be adapted for both Key Stage 1 and Key Stage 2 and has been used in primary schools from Year 2 to Year 6. Any text can be applied to the programme, fiction or non-fiction, reading scheme or 'story' book.

Sunshine Spirals and Starters, published by Heinemann, have proved particularly popular with teachers using the five step approach. Their structured key word progression and humorous and lively stories, giving scope for extension activities, are stimulating for children, their support teachers and their Learning Support Assistants. The books also contain non-fiction strands which can sometimes link with the theme of the week and meet the need to work on different genres. Multiple copies of the books, one for each child, will be needed; a matching Big Book can also be used.

Other reading scheme books that can be successfully used include *Oxford Reading Tree* and Ginn's *All Aboard*. 'Real' books reflecting the interest and enjoyment of the children and linking with the theme of the week have their place, but do not reinforce the structured key word or initial sound overlearning that is essential for children with learning difficulties at this stage. They can be used at the fifth step of the programme to highlight or reinforce a word or a rhyme and to help to put the skills learned into context – again vital for success.

The small step structure of the programme fits well into literacy hour planning as each day of the week covers a different activity for a small group of struggling readers. The five steps cover a range of teaching objectives from the National Literacy Framework; these are detailed in Figure 4.1. The objectives will appear on a group or individual IEP for each child; brief notes at the end of the week's activities will enable the teacher and support assistant to monitor progress towards reaching these IEP targets.

Many key objectives from the Literacy Framework, which are shown below, will be covered in the 5 step programme.

Word Level Objectives

- To understand and be able to rhyme, and to relate this to spelling patterns.
- Knowledge of grapheme/phoneme correspondences.
- Alphabetic letter knowledge and alphabetic order.
- Reading on sight (and spelling) high frequency words.
- Reading on sight the words from texts of appropriate difficulty.
- To recognise the critical features of words (e.g. shape, length and common spelling patterns).
- To spell common irregular words.
- To practise new spellings by 'look, say, cover, write, check' strategy.
- Writing letters using correct series of movements/form letters correctly/practise correct formation of basic joins.

Sentence Level Work

- To write captions and simple sentences, and to re-read, recognising whether or not they make sense (e.g. missing words, wrong word order).
- To use the term 'sentence' to identify sentences in text.
- To expect reading to make sense and check if it does not.
- To use awareness of the grammar of a sentence to decipher new or unfamiliar words (e.g. predict text, read on, leave a gap and re-read).
- To read familiar texts aloud with pace and expression.
- Learn about word order (e.g. by re-ordering sentences).

Text Level Work

- To use a variety of cues when reading – phonological, contextual, grammatical and graphic.
- To re-read a text to provide context cues to help read unfamiliar words.
- To choose and read familiar books with concentration and attention, discuss preferences and give reasons.
- To discuss reasons for, or causes of, incidents in stories.
- To identify and discuss characters.
- To predict what a given book might be about from covers/blurb/ title/illustration; to discuss what it might tell in advance of reading and check to see if it does.
- To predict story endings/incidents.
- To discuss story settings.
- To compare books by the same author.
- To skim-read title, contents page, illustrations, headings and sub-headings, to speculate what a book might be about.

Figure 4.1 Objectives/targets for IEPs

Day 1: Guided reading

Look at the book together. Spend time talking about it, e.g. Who wrote it? Who illustrated it? From the title what do the children think it is about? Look through the book together. Encourage comments and predictions. Read the book to the children, then read the book with the children, using the Literacy Hour guided reading approach, encouraging pupils to read independently.

Using a word, character or picture from the book, identify the initial sound to be learnt. Talk about the sound using the book to put it in context. Use wooden or plastic letters so that the shape can be explored. Teach sound/symbol, symbol/sound correspondence, using the multi-sensory activities described in Figure 4.2.

If the children have mastered all of their initial sounds, this section can be used for work on C-V-Cs or digraphs.

Look at the book again. Ask the children to choose their own favourite sentence. After the session you will need two strips of card per child so that you can write their sentence out twice in preparation for Day 2.

Look at the letter shapes.

Say and listen to the sound (oral and aural).

Finger trace around the letter shapes.

Repeat, then write the letters from memory, saying the sound.

Note. The child is not copying the letter but memorising it and then using the stimulus to retrieve it again from memory.

Additional multi-sensory resources

Sand tray
Feely bag
Wooden or plastic letters
Chalk board
Magic changer pens
Writing in the air, on their backs
Tracing
Playdough
Thick/thin paint brushes or marker pens
Corrugated paper for children to write on with paint or cut out for tactile
   letter shapes
Plasticine
'Magic Writer' – child writes on board and pulls tab to make writing
   disappear
Sandpaper
Finger paints
Coloured salt or rice
Pipe cleaners
String

Figure 4.2 Multi-sensory activities for learning initial sounds, digraphs and high frequency words

Day 2: Word and Sentence Level Work

Recap sound from Day 1 and previous weeks.

Re-read the book together. Encourage the children to remember their own chosen sentence. Put the prepared sentence strips on the table and play pairs games by encouraging the children to match the sentences and then turn them over to try and remember where the other one of the pair can be found on the table. Have the children read each others' sentences. Draw the children's attention to punctuation (such as speech marks or question marks) in their chosen sentence. Cut up one sentence and build a match under the complete one. Take a word away from each child's sentence, ask what is missing. Encourage children to do this in pairs. Write or stick the original sentence into a book and encourage children to write it again underneath using, look/say/cover/say/write/say/check/say method.

Day 3: Word Level Work – high frequency words

Recap sound from Day 1 and previous weeks. Identify the high frequency word to be taught from the book. Talk about the word and let the children make up their own sentences which contain it.

Teach the word using a multi-sensory approach. Reinforce using a resource from the suggestions list in Figure 4,2. Alternatively make the word with wooden or plastic letters, put them in a 'feely bag' and encourage the children to draw them out in the correct order.

Have the children make their own high frequency word card with the word on the front and their own sentence (illustrated) on the back.

Day 4: Word Level Work – rhyming, spelling

Read the book and use to highlight words to be used as the rhyming 'base'. Make up rhyming pairs or rhyming couplets, including silly ones. Children will often enjoy the challenge of who can make the longest rhyming sentence, e.g. 'A man called Dan put his Gran in his van with a pan'. The children can choose their favourite sentence which you can write in a group rhyme book and which they can then illustrate.

Put out the rime (in, at, etc.) and arrange possible plastic or wooden letter onsets on the table; the children match and say and then write the rhymes they have made on a word ladder or a rocket picture.

For children who have yet to master the concept of rhyme this session can be used for aural work, saying and singing rhymes, oral rhyming close, games such as Spot the Odd One Out, Which Two Sound the Same, or playing games such as rhyming bingo.

Day 5: Reinforcement – overlearning and recall of all activities

- Re-read book – opportunities for more guided reading strategies, check initial sound recall.
- Make sentence again – cut up second sentence and rewrite using, look/cover/say/write/check.
- Play a game to practise high frequency words, such as can be found in *Making Sense of the First 90 Key Words* (published by A. J. Hardwick, Wellington, Somerset).
- Reinforce high frequency words with further multi-sensory activity.

This five day programme is intended to be used for a short period of about 20 weeks. It gives some opportunities to work on text and sentence level work during the week, but children will also have opportunities for these activities in shared class time. There may also be time outside the Literacy Hour that the child can use to practise the skills they are overlearning: taking the book used that week home to read to a parent, reading the book to a younger child in school, practising identifying initial letters or digraphs, reading sets of C-V-C words, re-reading the group rhyme book and so on.

In the pages which follow you will find a standard planning framework for the five day programme, and some examples of how it can be used,

SEN groupwork in group and independent work time	
Monday	
Tuesday	
Wednesday	
Thursday	
Friday	

Figure 4.3 A standard planning format for the 5 step programme

Word	Sentence	Text
e.g. To secure reading and spelling of high frequency words.	e.g. To write in clear sentences using capital letters and full stops.	e.g. To reinforce and apply their word level skills through shared guided reading.

| **SEN groupwork in group and independent work time** |||

Monday	Introduce book. Talk through it to look at covers, author, illustrations. Use story vocabulary to highlight events. Encourage comments and predictions. Read book together. Pick out chosen focus – phonemic, word, punctuation, etc.
Tuesday	Children choose their favourite page. Sentence written twice on card and/or flip chart. Sentences used for mix/match, missing word, look–cover–write, reading each others' sentences, writing each others' sentences.
Wednesday	Re-read book to highlight chosen high frequency words. Use multi sensory activities to reinforce. Use oral cloze to put word into different sentences. Children make their own high frequency word card with own sentence on back.
Thursday	Look at book again to choose a word for onset and rime activity. Make up oral sentences and then use ladder/rocket sheet and plastic or wooden letters to reinforce by writing.
Friday	Reinforcement – remind children of week's activities. Ask child to talk about what they did. Opportunity for children to plan a 'fun' activity connected with the book.

Figure 4.4 Framework for the 5 step Programme

This example uses a book called *Super Diary*, from Ginn's Zoom series.

Day 1

Look at the book together. Who wrote it? Who illustrated it? From the title, what do the children think it is about? Encourage comments and predictions. Read the book to the children, then read the book with the children using the guided reading approach.

Initial sound 'p' – use multi-sensory activities to support.

Question marks – draw attention to their use in the text.

Look at book again and choose favourite sentence for Day 2.

Day 2

Use **sentence strips** for matching and writing. Revise 'p' with a silly alliterative sentence of words beginning with 'p'.

Day 3

High frequency words – 'see' and 'we'. Use these strategies from Zoom Teacher's Resource Book.

See – Find in book and write it on card, add two eyebrows over the two ee's. Make a sentence for back of the card, e.g. 'I can see six sad sailors'.

We – Ask the child to write the word several times in different coloured felt pens. Explain this little word can be found in three other words in the book – can they find them ('went', 'Wednesday', 'week').

Day 4

Rhyming words – *Park* (page 10). Read the sentence, talk about the words that rhyme with 'park' – make new sentences, e.g. 'I can see in the dark', 'You can see a spark in the dark'. Make a rocket or ladder with 'dark', 'park', 'mark', 'lark' etc.

Day 5

Choose from:
  (a) Re-read book; reinforce 'p' sound and the words 'see' and 'we'.
  (b) Use a second sentence for sentence strip activity.
  (c) Use Zoom PCM: in this case one which reinforces the story vocabulary by asking the child to read and sequence diary entries.
  (d) Guided writing activity: use the book to encourage the child to write a simple diary for a week of his or her life. Give help with days and dates, and provide space for writing one sentence (e.g. Today I . . .).

Figure 4.5 Example of the 5 step programme

5 Older children working at earlier levels

Margaret Hunt and Jennie George

This chapter is about how to provide for pupils who are significantly 'out of step' with their class. They are working between two and three National Curriculum Levels behind and are unable to participate fully even when placed with the least able group in the class.

By the very nature of their difficulties, 'out of step' children will not be working to the same learning objectives as the rest of the class. They should be working to learning objectives from a lower age group or even from a different Key Stage in order that they acquire a firm foundation of basic literacy skills.

The literacy needs of the "out of step" child can rarely be met entirely within the Literacy Hour, especially as the child becomes older and the gap between his or her chronological age and attainment widens. The child will need other opportunities in the school day to consolidate learning and in some cases to be taught specific basic skills. They will also need opportunities for writing that are not limited to 20 minutes in order that they can plan, draft and complete a task. It is vital that these pupils are not given the impression that it does not matter if they do not complete a task.

Self-esteem and motivation need to be maintained. Consider carefully the age appropriateness of the resources you are using. This is particularly important when choosing suitable material for the guided reading session. Supplement sets of books with other materials. Consider the use of non-fiction texts which many 'out of step' children find easier to deal with.

In this section you will find a resume of the type of difficulties which are common in the 'out of step' child and how these difficulties impact on the four sections of the Literacy Hour (Figure 5.1). To complement this there are suggested strategies for differentiation to address the pupil difficulties (Figure 5.2). The final section of this guidance gives some examples of resources you can use for Year 5 and 6 pupils who are working on Key Stage 1 learning objectives (Figure 5.3).

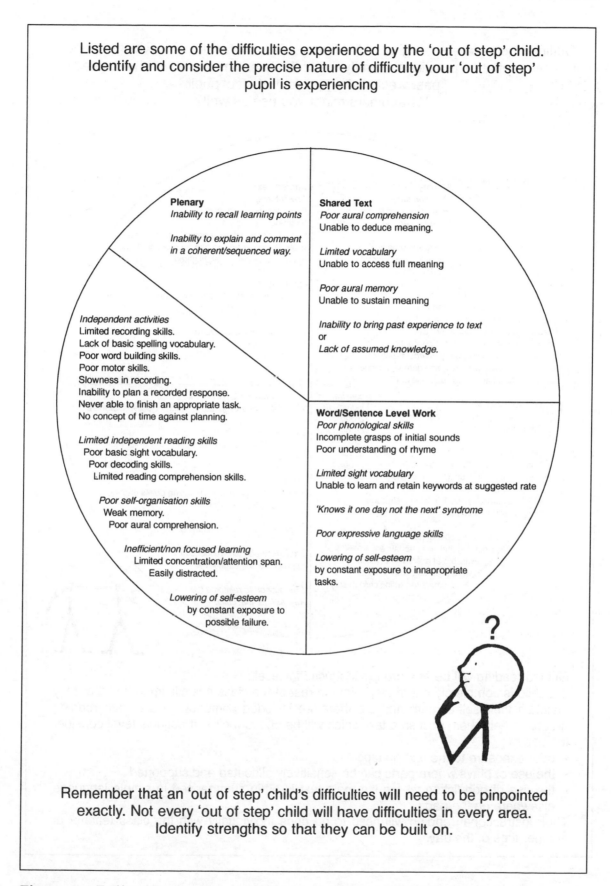

Listed are some of the difficulties experienced by the 'out of step' child. Identify and consider the precise nature of difficulty your 'out of step' pupil is experiencing

Plenary
Inability to recall learning points

Inability to explain and comment in a coherent/sequenced way.

Shared Text
Poor aural comprehension
Unable to deduce meaning.

Limited vocabulary
Unable to access full meaning

Poor aural memory
Unable to sustain meaning

Inability to bring past experience to text
or
Lack of assumed knowledge.

Independent activities
Limited recording skills.
Lack of basic spelling vocabulary.
Poor word building skills.
Poor motor skills.
Slowness in recording.
Inability to plan a recorded response.
Never able to finish an appropriate task.
No concept of time against planning.

Limited independent reading skills
Poor basic sight vocabulary.
Poor decoding skills.
Limited reading comprehension skills.

Poor self-organisation skills
Weak memory.
Poor aural comprehension.

Inefficient/non focused learning
Limited concentration/attention span.
Easily distracted.

Lowering of self-esteem
by constant exposure to
possible failure.

Word/Sentence Level Work
Poor phonological skills
Incomplete grasps of initial sounds
Poor understanding of rhyme

Limited sight vocabulary
Unable to learn and retain keywords at suggested rate

'Knows it one day not the next' syndrome

Poor expressive language skills

Lowering of self-esteem
by constant exposure to innapropriate tasks.

Remember that an 'out of step' child's difficulties will need to be pinpointed exactly. Not every 'out of step' child will have difficulties in every area. Identify strengths so that they can be built on.

Figure 5.1 Difficulties experienced by the 'out of step' child

Outlined below are strategies with which you are all familiar and which represent some differentiation practices. Identify the techniques/strategies you have used in the past weeks with your 'out of step' pupil.
What others might you use as well?

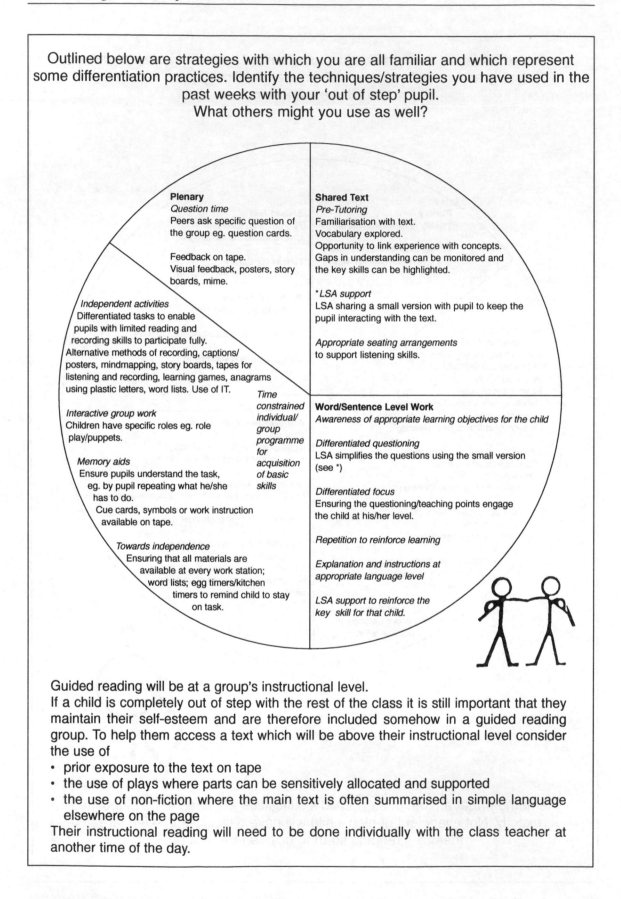

Plenary
Question time
Peers ask specific question of the group eg. question cards.

Feedback on tape.
Visual feedback, posters, story boards, mime.

Independent activities
Differentiated tasks to enable pupils with limited reading and recording skills to participate fully. Alternative methods of recording, captions/ posters, mindmapping, story boards, tapes for listening and recording, learning games, anagrams using plastic letters, word lists. Use of IT.

Interactive group work
Children have specific roles eg. role play/puppets.

Memory aids
Ensure pupils understand the task, eg. by pupil repeating what he/she has to do.
Cue cards, symbols or work instruction available on tape.

Towards independence
Ensuring that all materials are available at every work station; word lists; egg timers/kitchen timers to remind child to stay on task.

Time constrained individual/ group programme for acquisition of basic skills

Shared Text
Pre-Tutoring
Familiarisation with text.
Vocabulary explored.
Opportunity to link experience with concepts.
Gaps in understanding can be monitored and the key skills can be highlighted.

*LSA support
LSA sharing a small version with pupil to keep the pupil interacting with the text.

Appropriate seating arrangements
to support listening skills.

Word/Sentence Level Work
Awareness of appropriate learning objectives for the child

Differentiated questioning
LSA simplifies the questions using the small version (see *)

Differentiated focus
Ensuring the questioning/teaching points engage the child at his/her level.

Repetition to reinforce learning

Explanation and instructions at appropriate language level

LSA support to reinforce the key skill for that child.

Guided reading will be at a group's instructional level.
If a child is completely out of step with the rest of the class it is still important that they maintain their self-esteem and are therefore included somehow in a guided reading group. To help them access a text which will be above their instructional level consider the use of
• prior exposure to the text on tape
• the use of plays where parts can be sensitively allocated and supported
• the use of non-fiction where the main text is often summarised in simple language elsewhere on the page
Their instructional reading will need to be done individually with the class teacher at another time of the day.

Figure 5.2 Strategies for the 'out of step' child

Word Level Work

'Swap' and 'Fix' card games or CD-ROM, GAMZ.
'Chunks' and 'Making and Breaking' word-building games, Smart Kids.
'Paperchains', LDA.
'Track-packs, Highrace.
'Making the Short Vowels Work' games, A. J. T. Hardwick.

Sentence Level Work

'Breakthrough' (magnetic), Longman.
'Letter Box', Peter Le Feuvre.
'Magnetic board' word/sentence strips, Smart Kids

Text Level Work

'Writing Frames' and 'Writing Across the Curriculum', Maureen Lewis and David Wray, Reading Centre, Reading University.

IT CD-ROMS

'Wordshark', Whitespace.
'Wellington Square', Semerc.
'Speaking Starspell', Semerc.
'Ridiculous Rhymes', Sherston.
'My First Amazing Incredible Dictionary', Dorling Kindersley.
'Talking Write Away', Black Cat.
'All My Words', Crick Software.

Group Reading
Plays – parts at different reading levels

'Penguin plays', Ginn.
'Act One', LDA.
'Take Part', Ward Lock.

Instructional Reading

'Zoom', Ginn.
'Wellington Square', Nelson.
'Read-On' and 'Read-On Plus', Stanley Thorne.

Independence and Self-esteem

'Tips Cards', and 'Primary Tips Bookmarks', Basic Skills Agency.
'My Useful Word Book', and 'My Little Book of Lists', EPM Publications, 40 Park Avenue, Histon, Cambridge CB4 9JU.

Figure 5.3 Some suggested resources for use with Year 5 and 6 pupils working on Year 1 and 2 objectives

6 Managing behaviour difficulties

Jean Gross, Sue Jackson and Jocelyn Atcliffe

This chapter will help you plan for another very common type of special educational need – emotional and behavioural difficulties (EBD) – within the Literacy Hour.

Introduction

The literacy hour has provoked mixed reactions from teachers who have children with EBD special needs in their class. Some have found that the structure and predictability of the hour benefits such children, by providing a stable framework that helps them to regulate and manage their own turbulent emotional state. Others find that the demands of sitting still and listening during the shared time every day, followed by having to work independently while the teacher is occupied elsewhere, are too much for many children. The following examples show how the hour can impact differently in this way, on individual children with different needs.

Lucy

Lucy is a Year 2 child who has recently begun to present major management problems – pinching other children, hiding in the classroom, leaving the classroom and hiding on school premises, swearing and speaking abusively to classmates and staff. Contact with home has revealed a recent, bitter family breakdown. Lucy is the subject of a custody dispute and both parents are insisting on a rotated system of access which divides her time exactly between them.

The feelings which Lucy brings to school each morning – and particularly after each difficult weekend – are a painful mixture of anger, sadness and anxiety. She is on edge, and cannot cope with very much that is demanding of her mental energies. She needs order, calm, predictability, and fairly low-key tasks which for the moment do not present too many social demands.

The literacy hour has been a boon to Lucy. It has provided a safe structure where she can be fairly passive in the shared time and plenary, and work quietly a little removed from other children in the independent time.

Mark

Mark is a Year 4 boy who constantly disrupts in the classroom by wandering around, talking to other children when he should be working, and annoying them by interfering with their things. Before the Literacy Hour was introduced, his teacher had coped with this by watching him carefully and reminding him often to go back to his seat and get on with his work. If she had not noticed, other children would come up to her to complain about Mark's behaviour. The advent of the Literacy Hour, however, made Mark's behaviour very much worse initially. His teacher, occupied with a guided reading group, could not during the independent and group work time give him the frequent reminders he was used to; other children, conscious that they were not now supposed to disturb the teacher while she was working with a guided reading group, started to try and sort Mark out themselves. This would often lead to loud arguments, and the teacher sending Mark out of class.

Skills needed in the Literacy Hour

As Mark's story shows, the Literacy Hour poses particular challenges for some children because it makes demands on them to *manage their own behaviour*, in ways they may not be used to, and use a range of skills which may not be in their repertoire. In shared time, they have to be good at listening to the teacher and other children, sitting still in close proximity to other children, and waiting their turn to speak. In independent and group work time they may need to work cooperatively with others or to organise themselves for independent tasks, and will have to be good at remembering what they are supposed to do, staying on task, and knowing how to get help without going to the teacher. Figure 6.1 shows the kinds of skills needed in each phase of the hour.

In managing behaviour during the hour, the teacher needs to think first how he or she is working with the *whole* class to develop these skills. Then, for the individual child, thought needs to be given to pinpointing the particular areas which are causing problems. Is it the shared time which might need a special management plan, linked to the IEP, for that child? Or is it (as with Mark) the independent time which needs an individual management plan?

A further question for the teacher to ask is whether the problems are a case of 'can't' or 'won't' for that particular child: whether the child actually 'can't' comply because he or she has not learnt a particular skill which is needed (like how to organise the materials they need for a task, or how to negotiate with others when there are differences of opinion during collaborative work), or whether the child has the particular skill in his or her repertoire but is not using it – because the pay-offs for behaving in other ways are greater than the pay-offs for doing what the teacher wants. For Mark, we can guess that there might possibly be things he really does not know how to do – like how to remember and carry out a series of instructions, perhaps. More likely, however, he does know how to organise himself for work, sit still and complete a task, but is not using these skills because if he does not settle he manages to avoid written work (which he is not good at, and hates), and also gain a good deal of teacher attention (which he needs, but is not good at getting in positive ways). It will be more important for the teacher's management plan to address these issues than any underlying skills deficit.

For other children, the reasons for difficult behaviour in the Literacy Hour may be neither 'won't' nor 'can't' (in the sense of not having a particular skill), but different again. These are children who have learnt the fundamental skills of listening, organising themselves and cooperating with others, but who are under such stress in their lives that they cannot use these skills for a while. As adults, we recognise how when we are unhappy, anxious or angry our concentration goes, our tolerance levels decrease, and we stop being able to cope with minor irritations. The same things happen with children when they are troubled by uncomfortable feelings. Often the first thing to go is their ability to concentrate on demanding tasks, and the ability to work or share with other children. Lucy, who we described earlier, is a child like this. Although the Literacy Hour helped her by reducing the demands on her mental energy posed by working out changing routines and unpredictable demands, it also meant she could not cope with collaborative group work; her teacher had to recognise her emotional state and plan around this, being aware of the likely trigger situations which might spark off trouble, and trying to avoid these where possible.

Strategies for the whole class

The National Literacy Framework provides us with a coherent series of teaching objectives for children's literacy development. Just as important as this framework is the parallel framework – the behaviour curriculum – of teaching objectives for the classroom behaviours which underpin successful learning during the Literacy Hour. In order to help all children to learn, we need to plan whole-class strategies to teach these skills. The skills map in Figure 6.1 can be used to help with this.

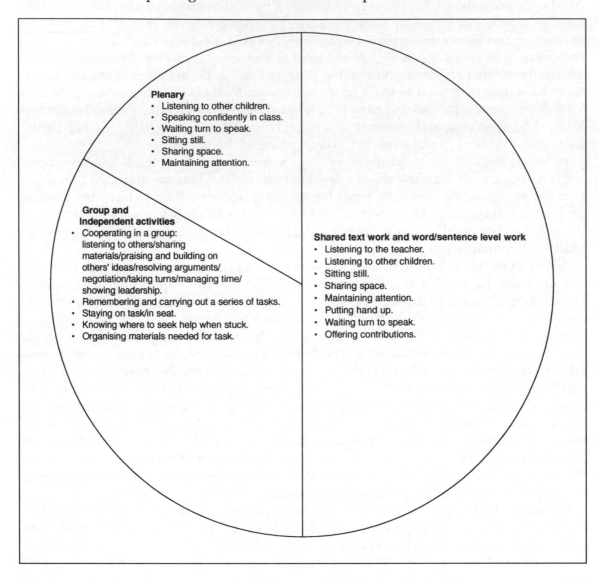

Plenary
- Listening to other children.
- Speaking confidently in class.
- Waiting turn to speak.
- Sitting still.
- Sharing space.
- Maintaining attention.

Group and Independent activities
- Cooperating in a group: listening to others/sharing materials/praising and building on others' ideas/resolving arguments/negotiation/taking turns/managing time/showing leadership.
- Remembering and carrying out a series of tasks.
- Staying on task/in seat.
- Knowing where to seek help when stuck.
- Organising materials needed for task.

Shared text work and word/sentence level work
- Listening to the teacher.
- Listening to other children.
- Sitting still.
- Sharing space.
- Maintaining attention.
- Putting hand up.
- Waiting turn to speak.
- Offering contributions.

Figure 6.1 Behavioural skills needed in the Literacy Hour

Rules

The teacher can work with the class to turn these skills into 'rules for the Literacy Hour'. The class may already have some general rules which they have negotiated for their classroom – rules about listening and keeping hands/feet and objects to themselves, for example. They can then be asked to think particularly about what they need to do in the Literacy Hour so that everyone can learn, and make a class poster showing their literacy hour rules, preferably illustrated and presented in a particular colour that the class have chosen as the Literacy Hour signal.

Then the teacher can start the hour from time to time by asking 'Who can remind us all what our rules are for the Literacy Hour?' He or she can get the children to demonstrate to each other how they would follow each rule, perhaps focusing on a different rule each week. At the plenary sessions, the class will not only review the work they have done, but also review their behaviour in terms of the particular rule they are practising. The teacher can make sentence strip cards starting with 'I liked the way that…', and give four or five of these to different children. These children then have to choose who they will give a card to, then read out, and complete the sentence: 'I liked the way that Alex listened to other people, in our shared time' or 'I liked the way that Karen worked quietly without disturbing people on her table'. The teacher can give out cards too, focusing on those children who particularly need them.

Rewards

For many classes there may need to be a reward system in place to recognise and celebrate behaviour during the Literacy Hour. The teacher can have a special literacy hour jar (appropriately labelled, using the chosen literacy hour colour), in which she puts a marble whenever she sees all the class following the particular rule they are practising that week, or – from time to time – the Literacy Hour rules in general. If the jar is full, there will be a class treat which might be extra playtime or a special activity on Friday afternoon. In this special time children might set up interest groups, working with children with whom they share a hobby or interest to prepare a presentation or a display. Or teachers might swap classes to share particular activities – one teacher organising a lesson where the children make fridge magnets out of bread dough, another running a dance or drama activity. Lunchtime discos, quizzes, using construction toys, going to help in younger classes can all be used as class treats in this way. Older children can have a literacy hour progress graph on the wall on which they record how well the class has behaved in the hour each day, with the teacher asking in the plenary 'How many points do you think we should give ourselves today?' and negotiating targets for the week with the children.

Ritual and routine

It will help children remember and follow their literacy hour rules and work towards targets if the teacher establishes a sense of ritual and distinctiveness about the hour.

There might, for example, be a special object (used only in the hour) which children have to hold when they want a turn to speak in shared time. In Key Stage 1, the teacher might lay out a special blanket for shared time, and remind the children that 'This is the time we sit very nicely and listen to each other: if we do this we can all get another star on our special chart on the wall.' With older children, the sense of ritual may be established by the routines involved in arranging the furniture for the shared time. One teacher, who works in a very small classroom and has to move a number of desks out of the way before the Literacy Hour can begin, has made a virtue out of this by having weekly monitors to move the furniture; the rest of the class know that their role is to sit very still, out of the way while this is done, and the whole activity is timed on a stopwatch with one child (a different one each week) reporting back on the time taken. The children try very hard to break their own record; the exercise promotes cooperation and gets the hour off to a good start.

Transition points

Many teachers have found it helpful to use a large poster with the Literacy Hour 'clock' on it: pointing to the clock as the hour begins and as it moves into its different phases again helps children to cue themselves into the behaviour that is expected of them, and manage the transition points, which if not carefully organised and planned for can lead to problems.

It is a good idea to build in some 'fidget time' at these transition points. Before children settle for the shared time at the start of the hour, the teacher can build in a short routine that will help children to relax – everyone shaking their shoulders, screwing up their faces tight then letting go, wiggling feet, moving arms quickly up and down. At the end of the shared time, before they move off into their groups, the same routine can be repeated.

Giving instructions

Transitions in the Literacy Hour mean lots of instructions for children to listen to and follow. The teacher can help the class learn to act quickly in response to instructions by following the 'Give an instruction and immediately praise two children who follow it' rule. Instead of focusing on the child or children who have not come to sit down for shared time, for example, the teacher will focus on two who have and immediately say 'Well done, Tracey, for coming to sit down so quickly', and 'That's brilliant, Paul: you came and sat down straight away'. The same strategy works well at the crucial transition to independent or group work.

Teaching the required behaviour

During the independent work phase of the hour, the next challenge for the teacher is how to keep the whole class on task while he or she is busy with a guided reading group or groups. It will be important that tasks are differentiated to recognise children's differing concentration spans: young children, and those who are still emotionally or developmentally immature, may need a carousel of relatively short activities rather than one long task. The class will need task cards on the table or wall to remind them of what they should be doing. They should have modelled for them the things they are expected to do when they get stuck; everyone should make a laminated and illustrated card showing 'six things to do before asking the teacher'; everyone should know the particular signals (like coloured flags placed on the table) which mean that the adult working with a group is not to be disturbed except in an emergency.

Prompts

While the teacher is working with a guided reading group, he or she can face the rest of the class and use a clipboard or more visible system (like marbles in a jar) to note, from time to time, children who are following the class rules for this part of the hour well – having previously discussed this with everyone. The teacher can set a kitchen timer for the end of 15 minutes guided reading, and give the whole class a point or a star if everyone is 'on task' when the timer goes off. The timer can also be set to go off at random intervals: in one class Year 6 children awarded themselves a point in a special notebook if they were on task when it went off. The teacher did not look at these tick sheets, but asked the children to add up their own ticks at the end of the week as a way they could 'measure their powers of concentration'; this proved very motivating and led to a much more settled atmosphere in the class.

Pupils taking responsibilty

Niggles and arguments between children are inevitable when the teacher's attention is concentrated elsewhere, but these too can be planned for. Children can think up ideas on how to calm themselves down when they start to feel wound up, including a place in the classroom where they can go to take some quiet 'time out' if necessary. In one school this was under a giant cardboard ice cube hanging in a corner of the room above a comfy beanbag; on the wall nearby were cardboard 'drip' shapes which the children hung up – one drip meaning 'I'm cooling off' but two drips meaning 'I need someone to come and talk to me to help me calm down'.

These strategies for managing behaviour in the Literacy Hour will work best if they take place against a backdrop in which discipline is seen as something which is shared with pupils, rather than handed down by the teacher, and where adults try to give children the confidence to handle their own difficulties and think out their own solutions to problems.

In classrooms like these things are organised in a way that allows pupil autonomy and builds self-esteem: children can access the resources they need, set themselves goals for both work *and* behaviour, and assess their own progress with the help of other children and adults. Behaviour is discussed by the class, as a topic in its own right, often in circle time: rules are worked out communally, problems brought to the circle, children encouraged to notice and appreciate each others' positive behaviours, and when things go wrong find ways of helping one another to behave better. In this climate the behaviour problems of particular children can more easily be tackled, with help from the whole class to back up the teacher's efforts.

Strategies for individual children

This section looks at particular strategies – variants of the whole-class approaches discussed so far – which have proved helpful for individual children with EBD during the different phases of the Literacy Hour.

Preparing for the hour

Children with EBD will often need someone to help them think ahead to the Literacy Hour and plan or practice appropriate behaviours. If only a limited amount of extra adult time is available, this is the most effective way of using it. The teacher or a Learning Support Assistant may be able to spend a little time with the child going over the rules the class have devised for the hour, and sometimes physically rehearsing them: 'Show me how you are going to sit when we do our shared time', 'Remember yesterday when you got stuck and needed to know how to spell a word; show me what you did that was so sensible'. Photos taken during the Literacy Hour can be helpful, with the adult pointing out the child listening well, or concentrating on a worksheet, or cooperating in a game, and the same 'Remember when...do you think you can do that again this week?' approach used.

The language which the adult uses in this preparation work is important. The emphasis needs to be on the child making 'good choices' about his or her behaviour. In one school all children are familiar with the idea of an imaginary 'choice box' which we all have in front of us: we put our hands into our choice boxes and pull out a choice. Sometimes this will be a choice other people will like; sometime it will be a choice which other people will not like. Children are encouraged to think ahead to difficult situations: 'What do you think would be a good choice for you in the Literacy Hour this week?' When they misbehave, they are reminded that they have not made a good choice: 'Do you think you could just put that one back in your box and choose something else?' When they behave well, people make a point of saying 'Thank you for choosing that behaviour'.

This kind of conversation can lead to the child identifying particular choices they want help in changing, and ways in which other children or adults can help. In circle time the child can be asked whether they can change a choice on their own; if not, and help is needed, other children may then volunteer ways in which they can help.

Shared time (Shared Text and Word/Sentence Level Work) and plenary

Many children with EBD find it hard to sit still for extended periods, particularly where they have to sit close to others. Ideas that may help include:

- Giving the fidgety child something to hold and fiddle with (like a very small squeezy ball) as an aid to listening.
- Making sure the child can have an active role for part of the shared reading or writing time: for example, coming to the front to open the shared big book or turn the pages; being asked to underline particular words or letters with a coloured marker pen on an acetate overlay; holding the pointer used to point to words on the big book or overhead transparency; giving out question cards, finding and fetching word cards from the writing table.
- Involving the child in 'whole body' activities where he or she can come to the front with others to pretend to be a word, a letter, or a grammatical ending – which gets moved around to demonstrate particular points.
- Using a special cushion or carpet square to sit on, or sitting inside a hoop – a 'magic hoop' which is likened to a force-field around the child, creating a space where no one can touch them or invade their space.
- Setting individual targets in negotiation with the child: 'Let's see how long you think you can sit with us in shared time today – we will try for 20 minutes, shall we? OK. If you can manage that then you will be able to put another clock stamp on your chart to take home.'
- Working on waiting to be asked instead of shouting out, or listening to other children without interrupting, using a joint problem-solving approach. The teacher might say: 'Andrew, there is a problem for both of us here. When you shout out, I don't get a chance to check if other people have understood, so I can't do my job helping everyone learn. And your friends don't get a turn to answer so they get cross with you. What do you think we could both do to sort out the problem?' Often this kind of joint approach can lead to a creative solution: in this case, the teacher agreed to call on Andrew to answer at least one question in every lesson, and more than one if he managed to put his hand up and wait at other times.
- Teaching and rewarding behaviour that will give the child something new and distinct to do in place of the difficult behaviour – holding an agreed class object before they can speak in place of calling out, or writing down an answer to a question on a clipboard to show the teacher later.

Independent and group time

This is likely to be particularly challenging for child and teacher, since the teacher will not be able to keep the child on task by frequent monitoring and praise, nor intervene quickly if things are going wrong for the child with his or her peers, and tension is building. Increasingly, the teacher will need to work with the child on strategies which will allow him or her to monitor and self-manage behaviour, and on teacher control methods which can be exerted at a distance. It may help to:

- Prepare an individual task sheet with the set tasks divided into small chunks – one chunk to be done in the first ten minutes, and one in the second. The child then sets a timer to go off after ten minutes and ticks on the task sheet if they have completed that chunk within the allocated time, then resets the timer, and continues.
- Agreeing a private signal the teacher can use (you could call it 'using the remote control button') to tell the child how he or she is doing. This might mean the teacher holding

up a card, while working with the guided reading or writing group: a green card for 'well done'; a yellow card for 'watch out, you may need to make a different choice'; or a red card for 'wrong choice'. The 'wrong choice' card can be linked to a pre-agreed set of penalties: every red card meaning five minutes off playtime, for example. Alternatively, the signal might be a simple thumbs-up (good choice), thumbs sideways and wobbling (make a different choice), and thumbs down (wrong choice).

- Using an immediate reward if the child avoided any wrong choices – being allowed to colour in a square or stick a sticker onto the special individual literacy hour notebook, for example, or earning three minutes Lego time later in the day for every section of the Literacy Hour (shared time, group time, plenary) successfully completed.
- Giving the child extra chances to earn credits towards a whole-class reward: two marbles in the jar when the child is on task when the teacher scans the room, as well as the one given to the class as a whole.
- Negotiating a private, agreed signal which the child can give to the teacher if he or she needs time out in the area of the room reserved for cooling off and calming down.
- Taking care to position the child in a non-distracting place in the classroom, for example well away from areas where other children go to fetch materials.
- Helping the child organise him or herself with an individual workstation. This could have a small folding card or balsa wood screen (about the size of a Breakthrough folder) which the child decorates: there might be a list of good choices for behaviour in the Literacy Hour, a photograph to match, or a place for a star chart. The child might also have a special clipboard on which to clip a task sheet, and a special pencil provided by the teacher to use only in the Literacy Hour.
- Buddying the child with a partner or a group of helpers, whose role is to provide support when the teacher is busy.
- Making clear that if the child has been off task, then the work will still need to be completed at another time, but choosing language carefully: 'OK, I can see you are having a tough time now and haven't been able to make good choices today...we do need to do this piece of work, though, so that you'll be ready to help make our book tomorrow. Can you think of a way of getting the work done before then?' Sometimes it helps to offer a choice rather than a directive: 'Would you rather finish it at lunchtime or take it home to do?'

Bringing it all together: managing the IEP

In this final section we look at how some of the strategies outlined above can be brought together for individual children – in this case Mark and Lucy, who we met at the beginning of the chapter – and linked to IEPs.

Lucy's IEP focused on keeping her as part of the class by minimising her stress levels. To do this the teacher made sure her classroom routine was highly structured and predictable. She used lots of visual reminders about work – colour-coded lists of group members, picture charts for class jobs, and an indicator board to show acceptable levels of noise for different types of work. The teacher used sound levels to manage the mood and let the children know that some activities need silence (such as looking at a book), some need quiet talking (such as group work), and some can be loud for a brief time (such as joining in a rhyme or refrain when reading a shared text). The teacher also did much work on helping the class use classroom or table-top space, and moving quietly from shared time to independent time and back to plenary. During independent and group time, it was decided that Lucy would not have to take part in most collaborative group activities, or if she did then she would have a clearly assigned 'safe' role such as timekeeper for the group.

Lucy benefited from these strategies and from the calm and ordered atmosphere in the class; her IEP could then move on to planning a safe, supportive environment for her in less structured times of the day – particularly in the playground.

For Mark the important challenge was to help him stay on task when not directly supervised by the teacher, and avoid winding up other children by interfering with their work.

Mark's problems were linked to his difficulties in producing written work, and the lack of opportunities he had to earn attention, praise and positive attention from adults and peers in school.

His IEP (Figure 6.2) identified three broad objectives: increased concentration, improvements in spelling and written recording, and improved self-esteem. Short-term success criteria were identified for each of these broad objectives, in negotiation between Mark and his teacher. Mark was going to be able to identify and talk about three pieces of work he was proud of, which he had completed during the Literacy Hour. He set himself the challenge of reaching a weekly total score of 15 points initially on a behaviour rating sheet which he and his teacher completed twice a day after each literacy and numeracy hour (Figure 6.3) to show how far he had managed to stay on task and in his own seat.

The IEP also targeted successful spelling of words with certain vowel digraphs, taken from the Literacy Framework objectives.

Strategies to help Mark reach these success criteria included using predictive word processing software to help him produce several pieces of writing, and working on 'Wordshark' to practise the target vowel digraphs for spelling. Mark's teacher made writing tasks easier for him by setting shorter tasks, and having him choose words to complete cloze sheets rather than writing independently from scratch. To help him concentrate during the independent phase of both the literacy and numeracy hours, Mark and his friend, Alan, agreed a buddying system. When Mark had concentrated for ten minutes at a time, Alan would put a tick on a 'Post It' on his desk. When Mark had earned ten ticks the whole class was awarded extra playtime – as a reward for helping him concentrate by ignoring rather than joining in with his attempts to cause a distraction. Mark also kept his own behaviour rating sheet: at lunchtime and at home time he completed his own rating of how well he had concentrated and then discussed it with his teacher, who added her own rating and gave lots of praise for good choices. If he reached his target points at the end of the week, he took his chart to a previous teacher, whom he very much liked, and to the head teacher, for more praise. He also took it home to his parents.

This IEP was particularly successful in bringing about change. By the end of half term Mark was doing much better and volunteered to raise his behaviour rating target to 18 points for the week, and then later to 20. He said that he felt much better about his work. Over time, the behaviour reward systems were phased out, and his IEP focused solely on a variety of 'catch up' strategies to help with his written work.

Conclusion

This chapter has looked at ways in which teachers can plan for behaviour in the Literacy Hour, as well as for the actual learning of literacy skills. It has described two kinds of planning: planning at the whole-class level, where particular ways of organising the class can help children learn the behavioural skills they need if they are to succeed in the hour, and planning for the individual child with EBD. The two are interlinked: the whole-class climate creates the framework within which individual children's difficulties can be tackled positively and collaboratively. Often, too, the individual strategies are simply differentiated versions of whole-class organisation and planning differentiation is the key for behaviour needs as well as for other kinds of special needs. It is to an account of how one teacher achieved this kind of successful differentiation that we now turn in the next chapter.

Plan No.

Individual Education Plan

Name: Mark L   **Year Group:** 4   **Date of Plan:** ___   **Date for Reviewing this Plan:** ___

Special Educational Needs Stage: 2

What? What are the broad objectives for this child?	How will we know? Success criteria for objectives.	How? Strategies/Activities/Programmes.	Who? When? How often? Roles and resources (who will do what, when and what extra resources are required?).	Date achieved/ Progress noted.
	By half term Mark will:			
Increased concentration	Have a weekly total of at least 15 points for 2 weeks running on his rating sheet.	Use of self and teacher behaviour rating twice a day plus praise from Mrs P, Mr K, parents if he reaches target; buddying with Alan – ticks on a Post It, class treat if he succeeds.	Class teacher, 5 minutes twice a day to discuss self-rating sheet; time weekly from Mrs P and Mr K to praise, etc. Alan will use timer/ticks in literacy hour to help Mark stay on task. Mr and Mrs L will discuss Mark's rating sheets with him each Friday – focus on praise for meeting target.	
Improvements in spelling and written recording.	Spell the common spelling patterns for the vowel phonemes oo (short), ar, oy, ow.	Wordshark programme within literacy hour.	Support/monitoring from Learning Support Assistant in literacy hour twice a week, on Wordshark.	
Increased self-esteem	Be able to identify three pieces of work (from literacy hour) he is proud of.	Use of predictive word processing software for writing; cloze sheets instead of writing from scratch during independent time of literacy hour.	Class teacher to differentiate task sheets.	

Signed

Parent/Carer: ___   Pupil: ___   SENCO/Teacher: ___   Support Agency: ___

Figure 6.2 Mark's Individual Educational Plan

Name: Mark L

My aim: To concentrate and not disturb other people.

My target points for this week: 15

Day: Monday   **Date:** 25 March

Literacy hour	Self-rating	Teacher rating
	5	5
	4	4
	3	3
	2	2
	1	1
Numeracy hour	5	5
	4	4
	3	3
	2	2
	1	1
Total teacher rating for day =		

I will rate myself and be rated for: Staying in my seat and finishing the work.

5 = Brilliant
4 = Very good
3 = OK
2 = Not so good
1 = Oh Dear

Figure 6.3 Mark's behaviour rating sheet

Section 2

Two case studies

7 Differentiated planning for a Year 3 class

Chris Waldron

This chapter is an account of how one Year 3 teacher differentiated her teaching for a class of children with a wide range of needs.

Introduction

Getting to grips with the Literacy Hour seems hard enough even when you have a class where few children have special educational needs. For me it presented a particular challenge, given that in our class of 26 children there were four children with Statements: a child with a profound hearing loss, a child with Down's Syndrome and two children with EBD – one of whom went on to a special school at the end of the year. In addition there were five children in the class who had learning difficulties and were on Stages 2 or 3 of the Code of Practice. At the other end of the spectrum, three children in the class were particularly able, achieving Level 4 at the end of the year in the NFER tests we use.

Planning for the class was a team effort: altogether eight different adults (including a speech and language therapist) were involved with the Statemented and non-Statemented children, and generally two to three adults were available in the classroom during each literacy hour.

We focused particularly on deploying our Learning Support Assistants to work with children during the Literacy Hour; they received special training at the Bristol Literacy Centre and have become very skilled at supporting the whole literacy hour, including both shared reading and group activities.

From the beginning we planned as a team for an inclusive classroom and an inclusive literacy hour: children were not taken out of the class to work on separate programmes, but had their needs met alongside other children.

Seating

The first thing I had to think about was how children should be seated for our shared text and word/sentence level work. Jonathan, who had the severe hearing loss, was reliant on visual cues. He always sat on a chair directly facing me and the shared text, with an additional chair next to him for either the teacher of the deaf or his LSA. Our classroom has large windows: we closed the curtains so as to prevent glare from the window, which might make it hard for Jonathan to pick up visual cues from my face or from the book. Georgie, who has Down's Syndrome, always sat beside me on one side of my knee, so that I could ensure that she was focused. Kerry, whose difficulties were emotional, sat on the other side of my knee: she needed the kind of closeness which you would get between a parent and a child sharing a book at bedtime. Then there was Jack – Jack, who most resembled the child in the Michael Rosen poem 'Eddie and the Gerbils':

Sometimes Eddie sits at the table
Sometimes Eddie sits on the table
Sometimes Eddie sits under the table.

I always insisted on Jack taking part in the shared reading but did not insist that he stay in one place for the whole time – something he found extremely difficult. Sometimes he would sit on the carpet with the group, sometimes on a raised bench behind the group, sometimes on a special soft cushion, sometimes at a distance, busily occupied but always attentive and ready to contribute an answer from wherever he was.

Shared time

We regard the inclusion of children with special needs in the shared text and word/sentence level work as a golden opportunity to extend their learning. The sharing of texts which they would not necessarily be able to tackle on their own has definitely helped them to develop new ideas and new ways of using language. In particular it provides an opportunity to extend children's spoken vocabulary: we always note new and interesting words arising from the shared work, investigate their meaning, and leave lists of these new words displayed over the week. Children work on putting them into families, writing glossaries, finding words within words and so on – using them to work on objectives appropriate to their particular stage of learning.

As well as making sure we all understood new vocabulary, I encourage everyone to participate and praise them when they do; we have found that they take a full part in the lesson – Georgie, for example, being like a little echo, always coming in at the end of each sentence in a shared text, repeating it after us, or getting very excited when she spotted such things as bullet points or brackets, and asking us why they were there.

The teacher's style of questioning is particularly important if all children are to participate. I try to vary my questions: asking a question using a particular technical term, then repeating it once or twice using simpler words. This is particularly important for Jonathan: for a deaf child, the subtle repetition is absolutely essential. It serves to protect the message for a child who, because of his restricted vocabulary, would soon lose interest and become distracted if he could not take part in the questioning that is such a vital part of the shared time.

Having Statemented children in the class, and advice from specialist teachers, has made me think about how I use language. It also makes me build in more recap and repetition within the lesson – for example, starting each literacy hour with a recap of the shared text, and reading it all through together again on Fridays. The good thing is that this benefits other children too, while at the same time I can stretch my more able children through the questions I use.

Guided reading and group tasks

I have five groups in my class, and make a task board for each week with five different tasks on it. Each group tackles one task each day. The tasks are essentially the same for all children, but are differentiated by outcome, by adult support, and within the task itself by varying the format of the resources the children use.

I make sure that for children with special needs the more difficult tasks come towards the end of the week, when they will have had more repetition of key concepts during shared time, and also will have been helped by hearing other children's feedback at the plenary.

For guided reading, I will select books at different levels for the five groups, but ones which are all examples of genre we are covering in the shared text for the week.

Name of school: Tyning Hengrove Junior School

Class: 3CLO 3SK 3PC
Year Group(s): 3
Term: 3
Week beginning: 15 June
Teacher: CW   SK   PC

	Whole class work – shared reading	Whole class – phonics, spelling, vocabulary	Group tasks (Letter writing – recount)	Group tasks (Verb agreement)	Group tasks (Spelling and definitions)	Group tasks (Collaborative non-fiction)	Group tasks (Guided reading Focus – letters)	Plenary
Monday	Recap genre letters, type, style, greetings, closings, new purpose – apology, differences	1st person singular/1st person plural, opening and closing phrases	A Letter writing — T OA I	B Verb agreement — T OA I	C Spelling and definitions — T OA I	D Make a non-fiction book — T OA I	E Guided reading – RSPCA reply — T OA I	Collaborative work
Tuesday	Informal letter Booking form of letter 'Dear Daddy' characters	Phrases to indicate time passing expressings and feelings	B Letter writing — T OA I	C Verb agreement — T OA I	D Spelling and definitions — T OA I	E Make a non-fiction book — T OA I	A Guided reading – letters from Lucy, Level 8 — T OA I	Collaborative work
Wednesday	Comparison – beginning informality postcards	Tense Person/verb agreements	C Letter writing — T OA I	D Verb agreement — T OA I	E Spelling and definitions — T OA I	A Make a non-fiction book — T OA I	B Guided reading – letters from Lucy, Level 8 — T OA I	Letter Writing
Thursday	Letters to congratulate	Exact meanings	D Letter writing — T OA I	E Verb agreement — T OA I	A Spelling and definitions — T OA I	B Make a non-fiction book — T OA I	C Guided reading — T OA I	Spelling and definitions
Friday	Review define type/styled letters formal/informal	Greeting/closing phrase New words from reading Expression and thoughts	E Letter writing — T OA I	A Verb agreement — T OA I	B Spelling and definitions — T OA I	C Make a non-fiction book — T OA I	D Guided reading Letters and applications — T OA I	Spelling and definitions

Figure 7.1: NLP Teaching objectives: Weekly Plan

While I am working on guided reading with one group, one other group will have an additional adult with them, but the other three will be working independently. We make sure that extra adult support is targeted at tasks the children will find more difficult and that we all work together as a team. Georgie's LSA, for example, might support her within a group of children one day, on a difficult task where everyone needs a bit of help; another day we might encourage Georgie's independence by giving her group clear roles in supporting her, while her LSA works with a different group.

I use my computer to produce task sheets for the children which vary in their difficulty; some are quite open ended, others might only ask the children to choose between two words to insert into a passage, or provide a ready-made structure in which they can express their ideas.

An example

Some work we did from the Year 3 Term 3 objectives illustrates how I try to differentiate tasks. In shared time we read a number of texts with examples of letter writing – formal and informal letters, letters of apology, congratulations, holiday postcards and so on. Word and sentence level work for the week covered some of the vocabulary and phrases used in letters, and focused on verb tenses and verb agreement.

Figure 7.1 shows my plan for the week's teaching. I managed to find a variety of books at different levels, all with the letter theme, for guided reading. Then there were four group tasks, one (a carry-over from the previous week) a collaborative task where children had to produce their own non-fiction book (see Figure 7.2). This task allowed children in each group to take on harder roles (such as producing the text) or easier roles (making the contents list or the front cover). A second task involved using a dictionary to find out the definitions of some words from the shared text, and learning to spell these words: each group had words of different difficulty, and was able to choose between a number of different dictionaries we have in our classroom – some simple picture dictionaries, and others more advanced.

A third task asked children to write a letter to a friend or neighbour about their holiday. I planned different formats (see Figures 7.3a, b, c) which provided varying degrees of support. For the fourth task, I again gave the groups differentiated worksheets (see Figures 7.4a, b, c): they had to choose the right verb form to complete a sentence, or label a picture with cut-out sentences.

Make a non-fiction book. Each person in the group must have a task to do.

Think about the things you need to do:

- Front cover

- Illustrations

- Back cover

- Contents

- Glossary

- Text

Figure 7.2

Funtime Camp.

th June 199

Dear_____

I _____ on a school trip. We are staying in a holiday_____ . I

like the _____ . I don't like the _____ . We went to _____

and saw the _____ .

Wish you were here

_____

Figure 7.3a

Write a letter to a friend about your school trip. Your friend was ill and could not come.
Here are some ideas to help you.

1. Write about your journey.
2. Tell your friend about the place you are staying.
3. Say what you like and dislike about the holiday.

Write your holiday address here.
Write the date

Dear

Figure 7.3b

```
                                                        Write the address and
                                                             the date here.



  Dear
```

Figure 7.3c

```
  Choose the right verb form to complete the sentence


                              is/am/are


     He _____building a sandcastle.


     We_____having our picnic.


     I_____having a great time.


     They_____going to take us canoeing.


     She_____homesick.


  Now put your sentences into the past tense
```

Figure 7.4a Pronoun/verb agreement and tense

Choose the right verb form to complete the sentence

is/am/are

He _____building a sandcastle.

We_____having our picnic.

I_____having a great time.

They_____going to take us canoeing.

She_____homesick.

Figure 7.4b Pronoun/verb agreement

Cut out the sentences.
Draw a picture of the beach.
Label your picture. Use the sentences.

He is swimming.

They are having a picnic.

I am digging.

We are making a sandcastle.

Figure 7.4c Pronoun/verb agreement

Conclusion

Planning for differentiation takes time. Even though once done the weekly plans and prepared resources can be used again and again, or shared with other schools using the Internet, they do represent a considerable investment of effort and energy. All this preparation work, however, pays off when the teacher can see children with special needs – like Jonathan, Georgie, Kerry and Jack – being included in the same range of activities as their peers, and as a result being included in the same social world.

8 A class of pupils with global learning difficulties

Margaret Tanner

This chapter is about children with complex needs and global learning difficulties. It illustrates the kinds of problems they may encounter in the Literacy Hour. It gives an account of how one teacher worked with her class to overcome the problems. This example may be particularly useful for teachers in mainstream schools who are teaching pupils in withdrawal groups, special classes or resource bases.

The problems

'Switch off'

The label 'complex needs' covers a range and combination of needs that are cognitive, physical, social and emotional in origin. However, in the context of the Literacy Hour the children share a number of common needs: language and communication; attention and concentration (frequently interrelated); spatial coordination and fine motor skills. The first two affect shared text activities and shared word work. The last two affect independent activities, in particular representational activities and written work.

Most of the children have a restricted vocabulary and poor auditory skills: discrimination, memory, sequencing. Visual skills vary but, like auditory skills, are frequently affected by attention and concentration deficits. Most of the children are very distractible, especially in a group, and especially in situations where the main medium of communication is speech.

With limited vocabulary, poor expressive language skills and underdeveloped auditory skills the children have difficulty understanding that printed words represent spoken language and very little hope of making sense of texts that are far removed from their 'lexical reference store'. In real terms this means that they cease to attend; they distract themselves and others, making noises, seeking diversions, talking, looking about. They fidget and fiddle; they lie down (if you are lucky), roll about or remove themselves to comforting spaces under tables or behind furniture (if you are not!).

Is there anything that can be done to prevent these children reaching for the off switch? What do they need?

First, texts used must be eye-catching and interactive to guarantee shared class interest and grab and hold children's attention: simple, bold, bright illustrations with flaps or moveable parts attract attention; 2D cut-out pictures that can can be moved from page to page and attached or detached help to sustain interest.

Any text used must be within the children's language experience and needs to be supported by activities that reinforce vocabulary and language concepts: Makaton signs and symbols; clapping, tapping, beating rhythms of speech; using 2D and 3D props; singing and saying related songs and rhymes; playing relevant language games; engaging in small world play, construction, model making; picture making, collage, role play and food preparation, when appropriate.

There need to be opportunities for repetition to reinforce concepts and vocabulary and to provide opportunities for children to make connections and to make discoveries about letters and words for themselves. Words and letters, spoken, sounded and written are abstract concepts. Every opportunity should be taken to to make these concepts concrete, 'real', and manageable.

Finally, without focusing unduly on children's weaknesses, activities should help to develop fine motor skills, spatial coordination and auditory skills, as well as to improve self-esteem and engender interest through success.

We can summarise these key principles in teaching children with complex learning difficulties as follows:

- the need to hold their attention in a variety of ways;
- the need for repetition and reinforcement of new learning;
- the need for an increased focus on developing phonological awareness, for children whose auditory skills are weak;
- the need to match texts carefully to the children's level of understanding;
- the need to make abstract ideas concrete and real;
- the need to develop representational skills and spatial coordination.

Looking for ways and means

'Switch on'

What follows is a 'log' of some of my experiences with a group of ten Key Stage 1 children with complex needs during our first few weeks as 'clock watchers'. It illustrates many of the key principles described above.

I begin the term with the comforting thought that, rarely is anything completely 'new'. the Literacy Hour may be a new *initiative* but, we have always looked at books, told stories, shared action rhymes and sung songs. We have explored rhyme (and rime); we have clapped and tapped syllables of names and high interest words; we have approached text through pictures and symbols as well as words; the children have had daily experience of a pictograph alphabet; they have learned 'key words' and personally meaningful words through a variety of kinaesthetic experiences and all within the framework of a language experience approach. The literacy *hour* may be new; the focus may be different; organisation may have changed but strategies that have proved successful in the past should work again.

Week 1: Getting started

My very first task is to find a text that will guarantee enough shared interest to engage and hold group attention. It will have to contain language that is within the children's common experience, to give them some chance of success when trying to make sense of the print. Eventually I decide upon 'Teletubbies' and print an enlarged version of the Teletubby song as our first shared text.

I indulge in a set of Teletubby beanbag toys as a grand launch to the Literacy Hour and make four cut-out Teletubbies to accompany the text. High interest words are names and our very first high frequency word is 'say'. The children have no difficulty highlighting Teletubby names in the text with lovely, bright red, sticky tape (which fortunately peels off easily!). At first 'say' proves hard to isolate. Most of the children perceive 'say hello' as one word ('sayhello').

They enjoy looking at published Teletubby books and comics during independent activity times and frequently spot and identify names.

At the end of the first week we write together. Our text grows: Teletubbies say 'Hello' to each child ('Hello Jamie', 'Hello Kelly') and now the children point to each word in turn with great success.

The termly topic is 'Ourselves' and I have always started with a unit on 'Names'. Where better to begin an understanding of the permanence of written language than with the children's names: 'Special person' name cards, names on drawers, pegs, planning boards, names used for data handling activities and circle time games. This time however, I will include Teletubby names and there will be an ongoing activity called 'Spot the Teletubbies' for fun.

Concepts of words and letters begin as we compare lengths of names from Po to TinkyWinky with children's names of 3, 4, 5, 6 and 7 letters in between. This helps us with the Literacy Framework word level objective 'recognising critical features of words, such as length'.

Week 2: A text of our own

Time to write a book of our own about the Teletubbies – a simple text, one sentence on each page (for example, page 1 'Po is red'; page 2 'Po has a scooter'). 'Cut-out' characters and 'cut-out' objects enable the children to interact with the text: they have to find the Teletubby, or find the object (hat, bag, ball, scooter) to match the text. The text can be changed, objects muddled and the children can help to restore objects to rightful Teletubby owners.

This time we highlight the high frequency words 'is' and 'has' with red sticky tape (*maintaining attention by active interaction with the text*).

The children match pictures, symbols and words to baseboards and sequence a combination of words, symbols and pictures to make simple sentences (for example, 'Lala is yellow', 'Lala has a ball', see Figure 8.1) (*repetition and reinforcement through familiar activities*).

We sort pictures of things that TinkyWinky and Lala like, have, see or do, based on initial letter sounds and weave these into an oral story. We look for objects and pictures of rhyming words to put in Dipsy's *hat*. We clap, tap and beat Teletubby names to a graphic score (*increased focus on phonological awareness*).

The children cut, assemble and stick Teletubby images; they complete Teletubby puzzles and lace Teletubby outlines (*developing fine motor skills and spatial coordination*).

They love it! They are 'switched on' to our literacy hour!

Weeks 3 and 4: Moving on

Time for a change. Reluctantly (because of the interest generated and maintained) we must move on. The Teletubbies stimulated the anticipated interest and the language level was right. Names were visually distinctive; and because the children are Teletubby 'experts' they were in control of the text and they were able to predict unknown words in context. A good start, but difficult to follow!

Repetition and generalisation are important features of work with children with complex needs, and planning must take account of this as well as NLS objectives. Because the text is crucially important I decide upon a book about the children (they *should* be interested in 'themselves'). The format will be similar to the Teletubby book, focusing again on the high frequency words 'is' and 'has'. However, this time shared writing will

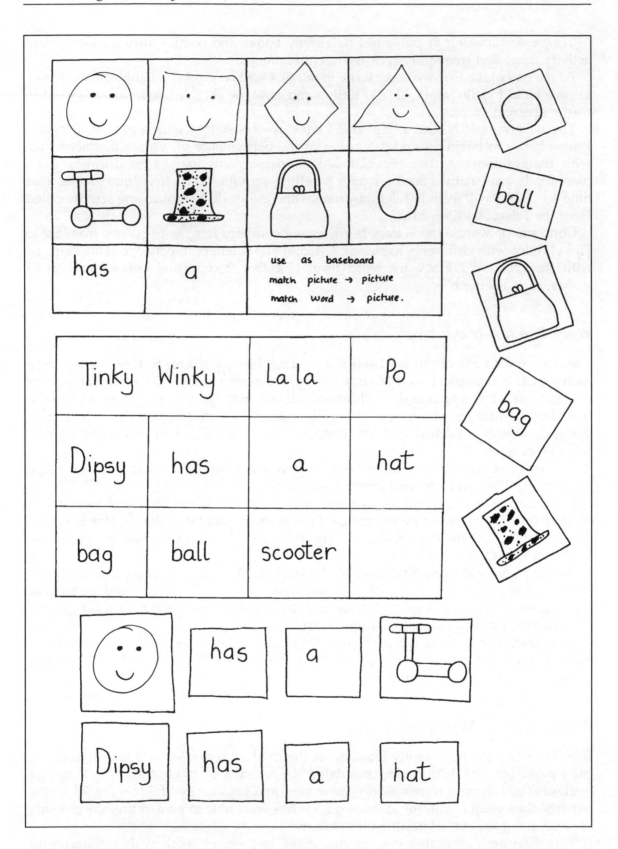

Figure 8.1

precede shared reading, we will 'write' the book together and then use it as a shared text for reading (*text based on language within children's experience*). There will be a simple pattern:

... is a boy/girl.

... is 6/7.

... has a cat/dog/rabbit/fish.

... has 1/2/3/no brothers.

... has 1/2/3/no sisters.

Shared writing, compiling the text together will address a number of text level objectives for the term. (See Figure 8.2)

PLANNING SHEETS OF THE TERM'S WORK

Objectives adapted from the National Literacy Strategy

Text Level Work

Reading

To track text in the right order, page by page, left to right, top to bottom; pointing while reading and making one to one correspondences between written and spoken words.
  To understand terms about books and print – word, letter.
  To recognise printed and handwritten words in a variety of settings – names, body parts.
  To locate and read significant parts of the text – names and speech bubbles.

Writing

  To use writing to communicate in a variety of ways, incorporating it into play and everyday classroom life.
  To understand that writing remains constant – will always 'say' the same thing.
  To understand how writing is formed directionally, a word at a time.

Sentence Level Work

  To understand that words are ordered left to right and need to be read that way to make sense.
  To use a capital letter for the start of own name.

Word Level Work

  To identify, initial, phonemes in spoken words.
  To read on sight, high frequency words.
  To read on sight a range of familiar words – names, captions.
  To recognise critical features of words – length.

Figure 8.2

A contents page develops once the children begin to use the book and want to find their names. We number the pages (for example, Kelly…page 9). They enjoy deciding who they want to read about and use the contents page easily.

A second book about 'Ourselves' follows. This time the high frequency word is 'likes' and the book is divided into sections: Food, Toys, Friends, Colours and, lest we forget, Teletubbies. These are again listed in a contents page, pages are numbered and different sections read on different days (*repetition and reinforcement*).

The first two weeks showed the value of interaction with the text through cut-out pictures. This time I decide to use cut-out figures of the children each holding the initial letter of his or her name, Makaton style. Brightly coloured speech bubbles stating preferences 'I like Pizza', 'I like jigsaws', etc. can be matched to the appropriate cut-out figure (*interacting with the text to maintain attention*).

The objectives for these two weeks include initial letters: the children are familiar with a mnemonic alphabet in which key pictures contain a visual clue to letter shapes. They can name a picture for each letter symbol and identify a key picture for most letter sounds. They now need lots of opportunities to *hear and identify initial sounds in words*, one of the word level objectives from the Literacy Framework.

An important aspect of work with children with complex needs is the provision of familiar formats. Regular activities such as picture/word matching to a baseboard: matching picture to picture; word to word; picture to word and word to picture is one such format. During these two weeks the children match words and pictures of colours, toys and food to baseboards. The words 'I' and 'like' enable the children to sequence simple sentences, e.g. I like jelly, I like red, I like dolls (Figure 8.3). An activity like this helps the children make one to one correspondences between written and spoken words and to establish left to right directionality, thus achieving further text and sentence level objectives from the Framework.

An activity like this is also endlessly versatile; it can be used over and over again with different vocabulary and sentence structures (*providing repetition and reinforcement*).

At the end of four weeks all the children can read each others' names; they can spot and identify Teletubbies; some children recognise 'girl' and 'boy' on sight and can distinguish between 'has', 'is', 'likes'.

Weeks 5 to 8: Growing confidence, branching out

Time to move on to Body Parts, the second unit in the 'Ourselves' topic. For the first time a published book is the shared text, 'My Body' (Heinemann). The contents page is familiar but there is also an index set out alongside a vertical alphabet. One of the children begins to sing our alphabet song and we are away. We make our own index in shared word work, using wooden letters and body part words, and an independent activity is born: matching words (with body part pictures) to a vertical alphabet. Now the high frequency words are 'this' 'is' 'my' and high interest words are body parts. We draw around each other and label head, neck, body, arm, leg, hands and feet (*activities guaranteeing shared class interest and attention*).

I change the order of words, introducing questions (this is my foot/is this my foot?) but it is beyond the language experience of all but one child so she does this individually as an activity and I store the idea away for another day.

Once again a language experience approach comes into play. Role play is a hospital complete with X-rays! The children make skeletons from rolled, white plasticene and cut strips of white paper; they print figures; they cut, assemble and stick figures, and make collage figures. We do body image puzzles and play 'The Body Game' (Dorling Kindersley). At circle time the children pass on simple messages to each other to touch

Figure 8.3

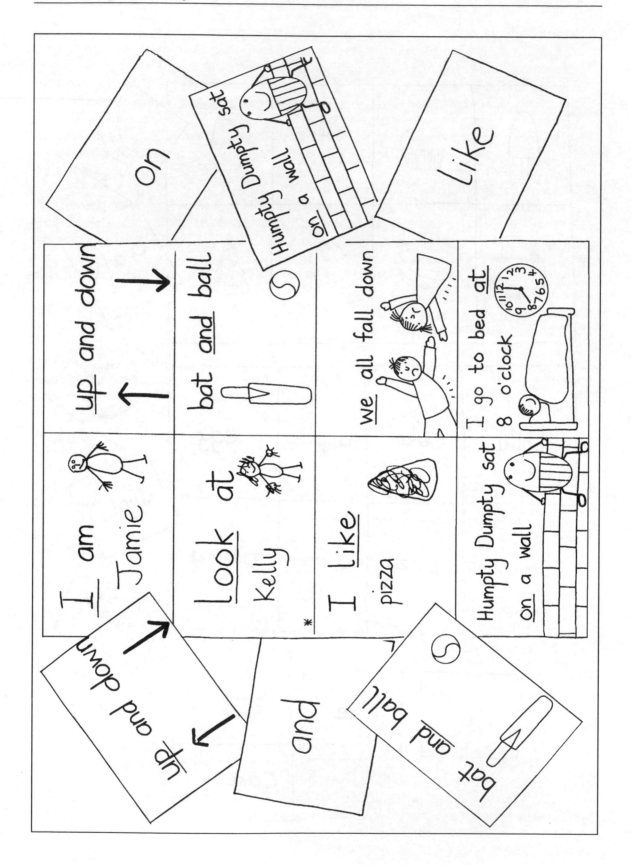

Figure 8.4

different body parts and, of course, we sing songs involving body bits. We use 'My world' ICT programmes about our bodies (*reinforcing vocabulary* and *developing representational skills, fine motor skills and spatial coordination*).

A new character makes an appearance – Skelly the skeleton. We write a rhyming book about Skelly using familiar high frequency words, 'is', 'has', 'likes' (*repetition and reinforcement*). 'Skelly likes Kelly. Skelly likes jelly. Skelly has a telly, Skelly has a welly'. The welly is smelly. We sort words: jelly, rat, telly, hat, welly, mat. We do this as a shared activity and all the children do it independently (*focus on phonological awareness*). Most of the children are able to match words to the pictures in each rhyming family. A few children are able to read the words in each family as a list.

A second book about Skelly is our last text for this half term – another home-made interactive text. Skelly loses a different part of his body on each page; the children identify and find the appropriate part and velcro it into place. The text is 'Skelly the skeleton lost his ... This is Skelly's ...'. They also find an appropriate speech bubble: 'my head', 'my foot', 'my leg' etc., and velcro it by Skelly's mouth (*maintaining attention by active interaction with the text*).

Once again we highlight 'this', 'is' and now we also find 'his' (*repetition and reinforcement*). I make up a song about Skelly the skeleton to the tune of 'Nellie the elephant'.

During the term a gang of hooligan characters have developed, known collectively as 'The Meanies'. They are the 'Letter Gobbler' (who eats the first letters of words – he will eventually graduate to final consonants and middle vowels), the 'Word Muddler' (who mixes up the order of letters in words) and the 'Sentence Muddler' (who changes the order of words in sentences). Whenever we have a visit from one of these characters we find a note containing a drawing of the Meanie and a message, for example 'Ha, ha, ha, I have muddled up your sentences. I bet you can't sort them out', signed The Sentence Muddler. The children respond to the challenge with enthusiasm, excitement, interest and fun. I hope 'The Meanies' will help to establish concepts of letters, words and sentences (*opportunities to have abstract ideas made concrete and real*). Most of the children can already spot the handywork of the Letter Gobbler because of the dramatic bites taken out of word cards. 'The Meanies' have provided a regular basis for word work activities and for some independent activities too. The children find missing initial letters; rearrange muddled sentences using matching word cards and sort muddled words using wooden or magnetic letters (*providing familiar formats*).

High frequency words

The children are beginning to recognise some high frequency words: 'is, has, likes, this, my' in the context of shared texts. We have a word wall display in the classroom for 'over and over again' words. New high frequency words are added to this as they appear in shared texts. The children will take home 'keyword in context' cards (a high frequency word in isolation on one side of a card; the word in the context of a sentence, with a supporting illustration on the reverse of the card – see for example Figure 8.4). Children who lose cards can have a book version of this: key word in isolation on one side of a page; key word in the context of a sentence on the reverse. I will also make small books for each key word we focus on, so that there are several sentences for each high frequency word. Children can practise isolating the word in the context of sentences. Baseboards for matching words, symbols and pictures can also be used to practise and reinforce high frequency words – an example is shown in Figure 8.5.

Each week the children will find and highlight high frequency words in texts. They will make up their own sentences and read them. They will have regular practise reading these key words in context. They will sequence letters in the correct order to

Figure 8.5

make the high frequency words: letters in a bag is a version of this in which children feel the letters of a known high frequency word in a bag; then have to pull the letters out of the bag in the correct order to make the word.

Conclusion

The pages which follow (Figures 8.6a–f) show how I planned some of the activities I have described above. The Literacy Hour proved a useful framework for my planning: I could do many of the things I had always done with these children with complex learning difficulties, but made sure that I covered all the key elements in literacy acquisition. The children learnt a great deal – and had fun at the same time.

Shared Text Work – Weeks 1 and 2

TEXT: Teacher made Teletubby book, used to focus on:

High Frequency words: say, is, has, a, ball

High Interest words: Teletubbies' names
hat, bag, scooter
red, green, yellow, purple

Initial letters: h, b, s, r, y, g, p

Rhyme/rime: '-at' words (hat)

Alliteration: La la, Lee, Lucy
Pictures of words beginning with 'l'

Repetitive phrases: .... is ....;   .... has ....

Special features: 2D cut-out Teletubbies
2D cut-out objects (ball, hat, bag, scooter)

Writing: Muddling sentences based on the text:
(e.g. Po is green; Po has a hat)
Sorting out muddled sentences

Figure 8.6a Teacher planning for a Key Stage 1 complex needs class

Shared Word and Sentence Work – Weeks 1 and 2

1. Select pictures of words to make a 'story' about Lala.

   Does Lala like **l**ollies or **c**akes?

   Did Lala go for a ride in a **b**us or a **l**orry?

   Does Lala like **l**etters or **n**umbers?

   Did Lala see a **t**iger or a **l**ion?

2. Using red sticky tape, highlight words that start 'l' in Lala's 'story'.

   Read Lala's 'story' together.

   As above select pictures of words beginning with 't' to make an alliterative story about TinkyWinky.

3. Find pictures of words that rhyme with **h**at. (5/10):

   Pat, cat, rat, mat, bat (fish, dog, jelly, cake, bus).

   Sort words that rhyme with **h**at. (5/10).

   Match words and pictures.

   Make **at** family words with magnetic letters.

4. Letter Gobbler!

   The Letter Gobbler has eaten the initial letters of Teletubby names and of ball, bag, hat and scooter.

   Can the children identify the spoken words without initial letter sound? (e.g. *ipsy, *o, *cooter, *all).

   Can they identify the missing initial letter sounds (phonemes)?

   Can they find the missing letter symbols (graphemes)?

5. Colour code names (Teletubbies and children).

   Match counters/unifix to names.

   Count number of letters in each name.

   Compare lengths of names (longest/shortest/same).

Figure 8.6b Teacher planning for a Key Stage 1 complex needs class

Guided Reading/Writing/Independent Activities – Weeks 1 and 2

Guided writing/reading with teacher

Match and sequence words, pictures, symbols.

Match pictures to pictures.

Match words to words.

Match pictures to words.

Match words to pictures.

Sequence words (or a combination of words and pictures) to make simple phrases and sentences.

Re-read the phrases and sentences made.

Children attempt the following activities with varying amounts of adult support from Learning Support Assistants.

1. Looking at published books/comics about the Teletubbies.

2. Tracing pictures of Teletubbies.

3. Colour, cut, assemble, stick Teletubby body parts to make a Teletubby picture.

4. Make Teletubbies in playdough or plasticine.

5. Lace around Teletubby outlines.

6. Complete Teletubby puzzles.

7. Make Teletubby toast (draw face in bread with thumb!).

   Make Teletubby custard.

   (Both activities with an adult).

Figure 8.6c Teacher planning for a Key Stage 1 complex needs class

Shared Text Work – Weeks 7 and 8

TEXT: Teacher made book 'Skelly the Skeleton'.
Skelly the skeleton loses parts of his body (his hand, foot, arm, leg, head, body, can be detached/attached with velcro). Children identify missing bones and re-attach them; together with a speech bubble that says 'my hand/foot/arm/leg/ head/body').

High frequency words: his, this, is, my

High interest words: Body parts

Initial letters: h, b, f, l,

Rhyme/rime: elly

Repetitive phrases: Skelly the skeleton has lost his ....

This is Skelly's ....

My ....

Special features: Velcro to remove and stick body parts and speech bubbles.

Improvised song to the tune 'Nellie the elephant':

Skelly the skeleton lost his foot and didn't know where to find it.

Off he went with a rattle of bones, 'Where's my foot?'

Writing: Labelling a skeleton for a wall display.

Completing a rhyming book about Skelly.

Figure 8.6d Teacher planning for a Key Stage 1 complex needs class

Shared Word and Sentence Work – Weeks 7 and 8

1. Put wooden letters in a bag.

   Children identify letter by phoneme or associate it with key picture.

   Match wooden letter to alphabet (written vertically).

   Children make an index of body parts, matching an illustrated word card to the appropriate initial letter.

2. Letter Gobbler!

   The Letter Gobbler has eaten the initial letters of body part words.

   Can the children identify the spoken words without initial letter sounds (e.g. ead, eg, oot, ody, and).

   Can they identify the missing initial letter sounds (phonemes).

   Can they find the missing letter symbols (graphemes).

3. Word Muddler!

   The Word Muddler has muddled letters from the words: the, is, my. They are in a bag. Can the children pick out letters in the right order to make each word?

   The Word Muddler has also muddled up some body part words.

   Can the children match wooden letters to the anagrams and rearrange them to make the words illustrated on the cards.

4. Find pictures of words that rhyme with Skelly (5/11):

   jelly, welly, telly, Kelly, smelly/rat, bat, mat, hat, Pat, cat.

   Sort words that rhyme with Skelly (5/11).

   Match words and pictures.

   Make 'elly' words with magnetic letters.

5. Make a collection of pictures of words that begin with the same sound as Skelly:

   Skelly likes sandwiches.

   Skelly has six socks.

   Skelly has seven sausages.

   Skelly sits on a swing.

   Skelly saw a spider, a snail and a snowman.

   Sort words for TinkyWinky at the same time.

Figure 8.6e Teacher planning for a Key Stage 1 complex needs class

Guided Reading/Writing/Independent Activities – Weeks 7 and 8

Guided writing/reading with teacher

Match pictures to pictures.

Match words to words.

Match pictures to words.

Match words to pictures.

Sequence words (or a combination of words and pictures) to make simple sentences.

Re-read the sentences made.

Activities with varying amounts of adult support.

1. Make skeletons using white plasticine (on black paper).

2. Make skeletons, cutting strips of white paper and sticking on to black paper.

3. Assemble and stick photocopied skeleton parts.

4. Label skeletons: using a combination of pictures and words.

5. Label skeletons:

    matching word to word;

    matching words to initial letters;

    matching words to body parts (initial sound only).

6. Sort pictures of words that rhyme with Skelly and Pat.
    Sort words that rhyme with Pat and words that rhyme with Skelly.

7. Make a concertina book, 'Skelly the Skeleton'.
    Completing missing body parts.

8. Look at non-fiction books about the human body.

Figure 8.6f Teacher planning for a Key Stage 1 complex needs class

Section 3

Specialist advice on lower incidence needs

9 Children with speech and language difficulties

Yvonne Wren

This chapter is about children with speech and language difficulties. It shows how their needs can be met in the Literacy Hour.

Introduction

The child with a speech and language impairment could easily be seen as the child for whom the Literacy Hour is of limited benefit.

'He can't say the word so how is he going to read it?'
'She doesn't understand spoken instructions yet so there's not much point looking at written ones.'
'He struggles with taking turns in conversation so he won't cope with group work.'

In fact, due to the close relationship between the development of spoken language and its written form, the Literacy Hour provides us with a useful framework to address some of the difficulties experienced by children in both areas. The child with a speech sound impairment would benefit from the phonological awareness activities in the word level work. Those with difficulties in constructing grammatical sentences in spoken language could be assisted by the sentence level work. Other children can be helped through the shared and guided reading aspects to develop their comprehension skills or ability to use language appropriately in conversation.

It is important to remember however, that the child with a speech and language impairment may also have other barriers to learning. Obviously, children with hearing impairments may have associated communication difficulties but those with visual impairments may also demonstrate problems with language development or using language appropriately in conversation. Pupils with either severe or moderate learning difficulties often present with a degree of language delay whilst those who demonstrate emotional and behavioural difficulties may have an underlying communication impairment. Children who have been identified as having autistic spectrum type difficulties have severely disordered communication skills. Those with specific learning difficulties such as dyslexia or dyspraxia often have a history of speech/language impairment and may continue to have covert speech/language processing difficulties even when the child is a clear and coherent speaker. For these groups of children, this chapter can be used in combination with the other chapters in this book.

Another group of children stands apart from these, however. Their speech, language or communication impairment exists in the absence of any other developmental difficulty. They may have a straightforward delay in their use of particular speech sounds or development of expressive language. Alternatively, they may have a specific language impairment which affects all areas of language development and has a severe effect on their ability to access much of the curriculum. Such children may attend specialist language units or schools but, with the move towards an inclusive policy in education, they are increasingly being taught in mainstream schools. Many teachers feel baffled by the types of difficulty a child with a specific language impairment may demonstrate and concerned at how to meet the child's needs. The literacy hour offers us an opportunity to address some of these children's difficulties, whichever setting they are in, and may help to avoid the plight of many such children – sitting quietly at the back of the class, described as causing 'no trouble' but making minimal progress.

Types of difficulty and implications for the Literacy Hour

Whether the child in your class has a speech and language impairment as part of a broader developmental difficulty or whether their difficulties are specific to speech and language, the areas in which they might experience difficulties are summarised in Figure 9.1.

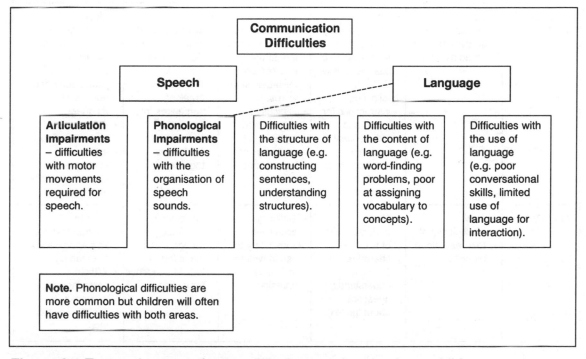

Figure 9.1 Types of communication difficulty seen in school age children

Many children will experience difficulties in more than one area and may also have difficulties with associated skills such as attention and memory. It may be necessary to work on these associated skills before beginning the Literacy Hour proper with this particular group of children. IEP targets can be used to identify these and other needs for children with special needs in the Literacy Hour.

All children with a speech and language impairment should have involvement with a speech and language therapist at some level. Access to such professionals is limited in many areas but where possible, teaching staff should use their speech and language therapist to help with setting IEP targets and with identifying strategies and activities to use in the Literacy Hour.

The Literacy Hour in detail

Given the variety of difficulties that a child with a speech and language impairment may demonstrate, it is reasonable to expect that they will exhibit different behaviours during each part of the Literacy Hour. Table 9.1 summarises how each type of communication difficulty might be demonstrated.

Table 9.1 Communication difficulties in the literacy hour

	Speech (Phonological/ Articulation)	*Language Comprehension*	*Language Expression* Vocabulary	Sentence Construction	*Use of language* Construction
Word Level	• Poor phonological awareness • Difficulty establishing grapheme– phoneme link.	• Poor comprehension of vocabulary • Difficulty assigning new vocabulary to concepts.	• Poor knowledge of vocabulary • Weak access to known vocabulary.	• Errors in use of verb tenses, word endings, prefixes, etc.	• Difficulty in using context to help read un- familiar words.
Sentence Level	• Low intelligibility of sentences read aloud by child	• Poor understanding of grammar in sentences (e.g. passive v. active • Difficulty following instructions for group and independent work and language used in plenary session.	• Difficulty accessing the correct vocabu- lary to use in a sentence/ mislabels some words. • Difficulty in appreciating multiple meanings of homophones.	• Use of incorrect word order. • Poor use of grammar. • Difficulty in breaking sentences into parts and connecting sentences together	• Uses language for limited functions. • Difficulty appreciating jokes, puns and non-literal language. • Difficulty understanding meaning of sentences in context of whole text.
Text Level	• Low intelligibility of text read aloud by child.	• Poor understanding of text used in shared reading. • Difficulty understanding questions about the text.	• Difficulty accessing vocabulary to use in writing or in para- phrasing	• Difficulty in translating thoughts and ideas into a logical sequence for writing.	• Able to decode text but little appreciation of meaning. • Difficulty using language to predict, explain, reason etc.

Word Level Work

The majority of children with speech sound difficulties have a fundamental difficulty with knowing which sound belongs in which word. Contrary to popular belief, their difficulty is only rarely due to an impairment of motor movement and therefore such children derive little benefit from instructions to copy particular mouth postures or tongue positions. Indeed, such an approach can be harmful and result in a child becoming overly aware of his articulatory movements or reluctant to speak. In most cases these children require work on phonological awareness – i.e. the skills which are required to develop effective phonic strategies for learning to read and spell. The literacy hour therefore provides us with a framework to help these children make progress in both their literacy skills and their speech.

Work on rhyme, segmenting words into sounds and blending sounds into words will all help the child with a speech sound impairment. However, it may be necessary to modify an activity or to break it down to a simpler level of processing. For example, the teacher's notes for Word Level Work, Unit 2 – phonics (page 21, module 2) suggests a teaching sequence for introducing children to read and spell C-V-C words. This sequence appears straightforward enough for most children but the tasks suggested actually involve a number of different sound processing skills which may prove too much for some. Table 9.2 provides alternative strategies for children who find the suggested tasks too difficult.

It is important to remember that children with speech and language difficulties usually have problems processing auditory information. They therefore need to make use of their visual processing skills to help them when their auditory memory or processing skills would normally let them down. As a consequence, it is important to

Table 9.2 Differentiation of Word Level Work for children with speech sound difficulties

	Suggested task	**Alternative tasks**
Identify rhyming words	Ask the child to generate seven words/non-words that rhyme with dog, cat, pig, etc.	Ask the child yes/no type questions e.g. does 'top' rhyme with 'mop'? Ask child to identify the odd one out in three pictures which you name where two rhyme and the third doesn't. Repeat the above task but silently – i.e. don't name the pictures for the child, ask them to carry out the task in their heads. Try words with no initial or final consonant first and ask the child to tell you whether they rhyme or not e.g. does 'see' rhyme with 'tea'? Does 'op' rhyme with 'it'?
Identify sounds in words	Ask the children what sounds they can hear at the beginning/ end/middle of dog.	Ask child to respond by pointing to a letter/picture symbol rather than by saying the sound (e.g. 'Jolly Phonics'). Start with words which begin/end with 'long' sounds (e.g. ffff, ssss, mmm). Try words with no final or initial consonant (e.g. what sound can you hear at the beginning of 'sea'?) Try identifying sounds in isolation if the child is unable to cope at this simpler level (e.g. which sound makes 'fff' – child responds by pointing to a letter/picture symbol). Give child pictures of words which begin with two or more sounds – ask child to sort these in to initial sound groups silently or in response to you naming them.
Blend the sounds into a word	In role (as puppet, robot, etc.) say the individual sounds of a word, (e.g. d-o-g), and ask the children to work out what the puppet/robot is saying.	Use pictures – child responds by pointing to one of a selection of pictures rather than by saying the word. Start by using 'long' sounds (like fff, sss, mmm); these are easier to blend than sounds like d, g, b.
Segment the word into sounds	Ask the children to take turns being the puppet/ robot and say the individual sounds of the same word, (e.g. d-o-g).	Use words which contain 'long' sounds to start with (e.g. 'sun'). Use counters to represent each phoneme – ask child to point to each counter as he or she sounds out each phoneme.

support word level work in the Literacy Hour with letter/symbol picture correspondences wherever possible and also to back up single word work with pictures of the target vocabulary.

Assessing children with speech sound impairments will often require the use of alternative means of responding to a task. For example, a child who consistently replaces the sound 'g' with 'd' in their speech may respond to the question 'which sound can you hear at the beginning of "goat"?' with 'd'. The teacher will not know whether the child has responded this way because of his or her speech sound system limitations or whether the child is confused about which sound they can hear at the beginning of the word. The teacher will be more certain of the child's skills, however, if the child is required to respond by pointing to a letter/symbol picture of 'd' or 'g'.

It can also be counter-productive to ask a child to name an item before identifying the initial sound. This will encourage a child to listen to his or her own production of the word and select the initial sound as they hear themselves say it. A child with a speech sound impairment needs encouragement to listen to others' productions of words and identify the initial sound that can be heard in their speech. At a more advanced level, a child could be asked to tell you the initial sound of an object/picture which has not been named by either the teacher or the child. The responses given will give you some insight into how the child has stored the target word in their lexicon (i.e. with the correct sounds or not).

Word level work can also prove tricky for children who experience word-finding difficulties. These children have particular difficulty in recalling vocabulary that is known to them. We all experience this 'tip of the tongue' state from time to time but for these children it is a daily occurrence and the meaning which they convey in their language is often distorted by their attempts to get round the problem through using associated vocabulary.

Children with word-finding difficulties have greater difficulty with new and less familiar words. They can be helped to acquire new vocabulary through the use of signing, gestures, symbols or other visual methods. The child is likely to have a stronger visual memory than auditory and is more likely to retain and recall new or less familiar words when each presentation of them by the teacher is accompanied by a sign, symbol or gesture. This becomes particularly important where the child has to learn technical vocabulary – the abstract nature of such words makes it difficult for the child to visualise their meaning as an aid to memory storage and retrieval.

Word level work also targets morphemic changes to words through the addition of affixes or changing a word stem because of a change in tense. Many children with expressive language impairments have difficulty with using different tenses, making plurals, adding possessive 's', etc. whilst others have difficulty interpreting the meaning of such changes. Work on these grammatical changes in the written form could be added to by targeting the same difficulties in spoken language at the same time. It is important to ensure, however, that the child has a concept for whatever is being taught before making too many demands on him or her in spoken or written language. The child who has a weak concept of time will find it difficult to appreciate the importance of past tense in either speech or writing.

Sentence Level Work

The teacher's notes for sentence level work suggests that one reason for teaching grammar could be because 'it helps children to write more complex sentences and therefore extends their ability to communicate complex ideas'. It is possible to substitute 'speak' for 'write' and use the sentence level activities in the Literacy Hour to extend a child's ability to communicate orally as well. Children with expressive language impairments tend to restrict their language to shorter, simple utterances and they will often make mistakes in the sentence construction. Many of the teaching strategies suggested in the teacher's notes (page 48, Module 3) can easily be transformed into oral communication activities, thus helping the child with an expressive language impairment. For example:

- Transforming sentences from: positive to negative; past to present; statement to question.
- Expanding simple sentences into complex ones.
- Combining and embedding phrases and sentences.
- Altering meaning by altering word order.

These activities are as useful for the child with impaired comprehension of language as for those with expressive difficulties.

Other activities are particularly helpful for the child with vocabulary difficulties. Work on strengthening the verb in the sentence by substituting obvious choices with more specific vocabulary helps the child develop awareness of the subtle differences in verb meaning. Selecting alternative adjectives, adverbs, prepositions and pronouns to fit in sentences can also assist a child in refining their vocabulary store, thus helping the process of retention and recall.

The child with impaired use of language for the purposes of social interaction can be aided through activities which highlight the different functions of dialogue. The use of language for metaphor, idioms and jokes can be especially difficult for this group and attempts to increase a child's awareness of these through the sentence level work is likely to help.

Writing activities at the sentence level can also be used to help children with spoken language difficulties. Colour coding of different sentence elements (i.e. nouns, verbs, adjectives, etc.) can aid children with word ordering problems. Symbols can also be used as a bridge into the writing process. Many children are helped through the use of a scribe: the resultant script can be read with the child, allowing him or her to self-correct his/her own grammatical errors in the spoken language.

Shared reading – Text Level

This whole-class activity can be difficult for children with language comprehension problems and teaching staff need to make as much use as possible of visual clues such as pointing and gesture to aid understanding. This part of the hour can also be used to develop children's ability to infer, explain and predict – skills which are difficult for many children, either because of the linguistic demands or an impaired ability to empathise with characters in a story. The latter example is often seen in children with problems of language use.

Shared reading provides an opportunity to encourage listening skills – teachers can deliberately make errors in the construction of a sentence or word. Children are encouraged to listen as they try to spot the deliberate mistake.

Guided reading

This provides an opportunity to consolidate some of the word and sentence level work plus an opportunity to address some of the difficulties relating the appropriate use of language for the purpose of interaction. Children with difficulties in this area often have problems in identifying the meaning communicated through language. They may concentrate on trivial matters and miss the key message which is being conveyed. Guided reading activities can be used to help such a child identify the characters and key events in a piece of text and discuss what the characters might be feeling in response to events.

Independent activities

Some children may struggle with this part of the Literacy Hour because of their difficulty with maintaining attention to a particular task. For these children it may be necessary to work on developing their skills of concentration before any of the independent work time can be of much use. For those children who are able to maintain at least a limited amount of attention, the time can be used for activities such as sequencing work. This helps the child with a speech and language impairment to organise their thoughts and ideas into a coherent and logical sequence thus enabling the listener to understand their message. Such activities can be carried out using picture material, possibly related to the shared text.

Independent activities could also include work on concept/vocabulary mapping. The child could be asked to draw a number of different pictures/write words (depending on level) which relate in some way to the target vocabulary from the shared text. The words selected could relate because they mean the same, or because they mean the opposite or because they describe the target word in some way.

Group work

Group work allows for further attention to the use of language for the purposes of interaction. Children with problems of language use often have a tendency to wander from the main topic of conversation, choosing to talk about something which has little or no relevance to the previous speaker's comment. Group work provides an opportunity for the adult to bring this to the attention of the child in question, thank him for his contribution but remind him of the current topic of conversation. There is also an opportunity to work on children's turntaking skills, eye contact, and other non-verbal communication strategies which these children often find so difficult.

Plenary

It is important that children with speech, language and communication impairments are given opportunities to feed back during the plenary session but there may be genuine concern on the part of the teacher that he or she will have difficulty understanding the child. Offering the child alternatives rather than asking him or her an open question can reduce this possibility. For example, 'Did you draw rhyming pictures or arrange the sequencing pictures?' – this not only cues the teacher into what the potential answer may be but also offers the child a framework for his or her response.

Planning

Figure 9.2 shows how a support teacher has used many of the ideas for the whole-class and independent time within the Literacy Hour to plan differentiation for a child with speech and language difficulties.

Conclusion

There are many ways in which children with speech and language impairments might experience difficulties in the Literacy Hour but there are also ways in which they may benefit from it. Moreover, the links between spoken and written language development mean that the Literacy Hour can be used to target both areas for those children who need it. However, some children who have severe problems with speech and language development and others with milder delays but who are in the early years of schooling may find even the reception level work too demanding. Such children require an orally based curriculum which emphasises listening skills and aims to increase children's awareness of the language they hear and use throughout the school day. They need assistance to reach a level of linguistic and cognitive development which allows them to access the early stages detailed in the framework for teaching. The literacy hour provides many useful strategies for working with this particular group of children but the need for effective differentiation continues, particularly for children who have difficulties with language – the medium of instruction throughout their school day.

Figure 9.2 Example of a literacy hour plan which includes the speech and language impaired child

Learning Objectives: (from Framework):	To organise ideas for story telling. To learn new vocabulary and develop phonological awareness.		
Class:	**Year: 2**	**Term: 1**	
	Task	**The speech and language impaired child**	**Resources**
Shared reading and writing	Read first half of this week's fictional text.	Ask child to retell events in story so far. Ask child to predict what might happen next. Use signs and gestures to facilitate compre-hension of text.	Pictures of text without writing. Makaton, Signalong, or other sign system.
Whole-class phonics, spelling, vocabulary and grammar	To identify new and less familiar words from the text. To identify the initial consonant in each of these words.	Help child to consolidate meaning by discussing similarities and differences with other related words. Use sound/symbol pictures plus gesture, ask child to point to initial consonant from a small selection.	White/black board to draw concept/vocabulary map. e.g. Jolly Phonics.
Group work	To paraphrase the text which has been read so far, taking note of grammatical rules for tense and number.	Act as scribe and read back to child asking them to identify parts that sound 'funny' and help child to self-correct.	
Independent work	Generating rhyming words for specific vocabulary from the text.	Use pictures of the vocabulary plus a picture of a rhyming word for each one. Ask child to pair the pictures up into rhyming sets.	Sets of rhyming pictures.
Plenary	Feedback from the small group activities.	Offer verbal choices to help child formulate response (e.g. 'were you working on rhyming words or correcting your story?').	

10 Children with hearing losses

Sue Young, Helen Walter, Peter Fudge, Ros Way and Ann Berger

The chapter is about problems which deaf or hearing impaired children may experience in the Literacy Hour. The first section looks at some classroom stratergies to assist the teacher in including these children within the Literacy Hour. The second section identifies particular issues for sign bilingual learners.

Problems

Seating – is there enough room? Can everyone see clearly?

Light source – if the light is behind you it may be difficult to see your face clearly.

Noise sources – is there a noisy heater or buzzing light? These noises may seem insignificant to you but can sound louder through a hearing aid and make listening difficult.

Suggestions

If the child uses a radio aid, make sure it is switched on and working.

Ensure child is seated in the best position to see the teacher and the other children, but not so close that they have to crane their neck to see your face to lipread.

Try to ensure that the main light source (usually the window) is behind the child so that it lights up your face. This will make it easier for the child to lipread.

Make sure the door is shut (window too if it is noisy outside). Get buzzing lights attended to. If possible turn off noisy heaters or seat child as far away as possible.

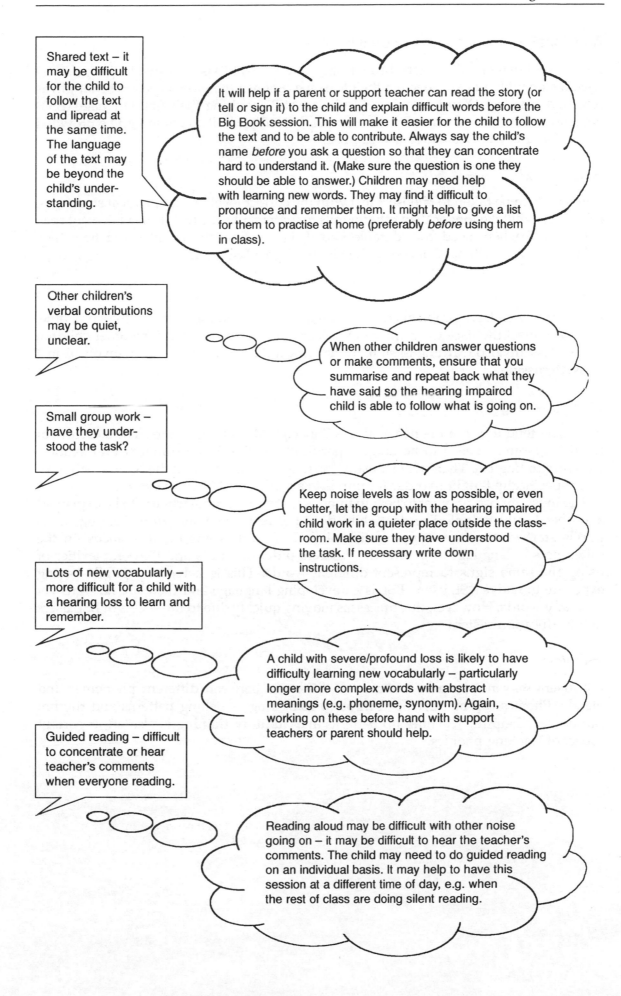

Shared text – it may be difficult for the child to follow the text and lipread at the same time. The language of the text may be beyond the child's under-standing.

It will help if a parent or support teacher can read the story (or tell or sign it) to the child and explain difficult words before the Big Book session. This will make it easier for the child to follow the text and to be able to contribute. Always say the child's name *before* you ask a question so that they can concentrate hard to understand it. (Make sure the question is one they should be able to answer.) Children may need help with learning new words. They may find it difficult to pronounce and remember them. It might help to give a list for them to practise at home (preferably *before* using them in class).

Other children's verbal contributions may be quiet, unclear.

When other children answer questions or make comments, ensure that you summarise and repeat back what they have said so the hearing impaired child is able to follow what is going on.

Small group work – have they under-stood the task?

Keep noise levels as low as possible, or even better, let the group with the hearing impaired child work in a quieter place outside the class-room. Make sure they have understood the task. If necessary write down instructions.

Lots of new vocabulary – more difficult for a child with a hearing loss to learn and remember.

A child with severe/profound loss is likely to have difficulty learning new vocabulary – particularly longer more complex words with abstract meanings (e.g. phoneme, synonym). Again, working on these before hand with support teachers or parent should help.

Guided reading – difficult to concentrate or hear teacher's comments when everyone reading.

Reading aloud may be difficult with other noise going on – it may be difficult to hear the teacher's comments. The child may need to do guided reading on an individual basis. It may help to have this session at a different time of day, e.g. when the rest of class are doing silent reading.

Additional issues for sign bilingual learners

For many sign biligual learners, British Sign Language (BSL) is their first language. They need a sign bilingual approach in their learning. English therefore needs to be taught as a second language. Younger children, who are still acquiring their first language (BSL) need to concentrate on using BSL to access early reading skills. This should be provided by deaf adults who are native users of BSL.

Shared text

Care needs to be taken to choose a text with the correct level of grammatical structures. BSL users will take longer than other pupils to understand the text if they have not seen it before. Teachers need considerable knowledge of English and BSL and how they differ. The child will need access to the text through a BSL user.

Guided reading

Pupils may well have problems focusing on the text and on the signer at the same time. This will affect the pace the pupil can work at. This can be helped if the other children in the class are also learning to sign. In that way a BSL user can really be involved in a class discussion.

Guided writing

BSL users tend to write English as if it is BSL, e.g. 'Mummy go shop'. The structure of English grammar needs to be taught specifically as BSL has a different grammatical structure to English. There will be many learning objectives not in the NLS which have to be specifically taught in order for pupils to access the whole framework.

The most important point to bear in mind is that new vocabulary has to be explained and specifically taught. The deaf child does not learn language from hearing it. As pupils start to acquire communication skills in BSL it is important to focus on the differences in language structure, the different order of words and the complexities of using the same signs to represent different words. This is helped by pupils having exposure to native BSL users. BSL is a developing language and there are no signs yet for many words. However, this process is moving quickly due to the sucess of BSL users in the education system.

Phonics

BSL users may not be able to hear the difference between different phonemes and blends. Phonics can be developed through using finger spelling patterns and rhythm can be very helpful. Teaching lip patterns and auditory training is also an important aspect of teaching phonics.

11 Pupils with vision impairment

Sue Rogers and Joao Roe

This chapter is about children with vision impairment. It describes the implications of the Literacy Hour for these children, and ways in which they can be supported in shared, group and independent work.

Introduction

As a result of inclusive education children with a wide range of vision impairment now attend mainstream schools and participate in the Literacy Hour.

The key aim of the National Literacy Strategy, that children should learn to 'read and write with confidence, fluency and understanding', also applies to children with impaired vision. However, the process differs in a number of crucial aspects.

Children entering school with a vision impairment bring with them a variety of experiences but they all share limited access to visual information, and this limited access to visual information is also likely to impair their conceptual understanding. A sighted child is continuously receiving visual information about the environment and much learning takes place incidentally. A young child without vision visiting a supermarket may not be aware of the variety of items available, the actions taking place or that they are surrounded by a mass of print. On the other hand, a child with low vision may perceive some of these aspects and form concepts based only of fragmented experiences.

Although a child may have developed excellent expressive language, it should not be assumed that this shows a complete understanding of concepts. A young child who enthusiastically describes different parts of a car may not know that these are put together to produce movement.

The term 'vision impairment' covers a wide range of conditions. The most severely affected child will not be able to see and will need to learn through other senses. Individuals vary in the way they cope with their eye condition and some children have a combination of conditions. Some conditions affect distance vision, so accessing information during shared activities will be difficult. Other conditions affect near vision and individual or guided reading and writing will present challenges.

In this chapter we will be referring to children with a vision impairment without other major disabilities.

Implications for the Literacy Hour

At the core of the Literacy Hour is whole-class teaching and shared learning. Learning in this way presents real disadvantages to children who find the mechanics of reading and writing tiring and are unable to process the information at the same speed as the rest of the class. However there are benefits to learning as part of a group and the interactive social process is viewed as significant in the acquisition of literacy skill. Taking part in group situations allows children to pick up ideas and opinions of those who share eir social contexts. Like all children, those with vision impairment also benefit from the opportunities presented in the shared time for the teacher to extend pupils' knowledge beyond their current level of achievement.

A key impact of the Literacy Hour is that a routine is established and children may become familiar with the format of the session and what is expected of them throughout the primary years. This should help promote confidence and independence.

Children with vision impairments can learn to read and write using enlarged print, Braille or Moon. Children with severe vision impairment require additional teaching and materials and are usually supported by extra adults, including a teacher of the visually impaired and a Learning Support Assistant. To include children with vision impairment in the Literacy Hour, regular liaison and planning meetings between the class teacher and the support team are crucial. Commitment of time is significant and the quality of inclusion relies on two-way communication. This should include, as a minimum, information about planned activities from the class teacher and the advice and adaptations to be provided by the support team.

It is not always possible to adapt materials in advance; for example, when an activity is based on a recent piece of a child's own writing. A system needs to be in place which enables the support team to provide, at short notice, Braille, enlarged print or word processed versions of the text. In practise this may have to be done at playtime, registration or assembly. Activities that evolve during a session using the children's examples and ideas will need to be adapted on the spot.

The literacy hour promotes group learning with the aim of supporting all children so they are able to participate confidently. Children learn both from the teacher and the contributions of other children. Contributing to a group involves a complex set of skills such as being able to interpret facial expressions, understanding when it is appropriate to make a contribution and when it is another child's turn. These abilities rely on vision, and children who cannot use visual cues need to rely more heavily on listening skills, and verbal explanations. The processing of the information also takes longer, so there is a possibility that some children will always be struggling to keep up, with a potential effect on confidence and self-esteem.

Children with vision impairment need more time than an hour a day to learn basic literacy skills. They have a range of skills to learn over and above the ones that have been modelled and taught during the Literacy Hour. For example, Braille users need to learn about contractions and when to use them, they may need some pre- and post-tutoring to understand and consolidate concepts. A child with limited vision may need extra practise and time to learn, for example, how to form a letter, use scanning and select from contents and index pages.

For some children information and communication technology will be essential for them to access the Literacy Hour. Due to their low vision, some children are not able to read back their own handwriting and rely on accessing a word processor; others may use an encyclopaedia on a CD-ROM to access information that is unavailable to them through books; Braille users will need technology to produce a print version of their work.

It is important that children are not overloaded, because mobility, word processing, independence, listening and social skills are also curriculum areas that may have to be fitted into a school week.

The Literacy Hour in detail

Shared reading

Shared reading is a whole-class activity. The teacher models reading from a text at an instructional level, i.e. above the independent reading ability of most of the group.

Children can see and hear the text and are taught a range of reading strategies. The sessions are intended to be highly interactive with opportunities for individuals to offer their reactions to the text. In order not to be disadvantaged during shared reading the child with low vision must be able to access the text, the teacher's modelling and process the information.

One obvious solution when including children with impaired vision is to provide them with their own copy of the text. This strategy works well if the child can still access the modelling provided by the teacher. For some children reading their own Braille or print copy may be a different process to following the class copy and they need extra input to follow what the class is reading.

Planning for individual children

Materials. Commercially produced big books are useful aids if they are produced with a clear font, using good contrast and spacing. A small book that is visually cluttered will not improve with enlargement. Pointers can help the whole group follow the text at the same speed but obviously the pointer should not obscure the words. This is vital for a child who is sitting close to the front and looking up at the print. Using a pointer from above rather than below the words may help overcome this difficulty.

The use of different coloured pens and the colour of the background board or paper will vary with individual need but good contrast and clear writing will benefit the whole group (e.g. black on white or yellow).

Adaptations. A range of adaptations may be appropriate for the same child depending on what is being taught, how fast and in what detail they need to process the information. For example, a child with low visions may need access to their own copy of the 'big' book when asked to find different features in the layout of a book, a word processed version of the text to find specific answers in a non-fiction book, or the support of an adult to locate key words and phrases.

Pre-tutoring. Presenting the book, a book of the same genre or looking in detail at the context beforehand can be a useful strategy. It is important that the child is helped to access the group session.

Comprehension. Concepts that rely on vision need to be explained or experienced before the session or they will prevent or limit understanding. Some highly visual concepts present difficulties, such as the story of Perseus encountered by a Year 4 child who is blind and has no understanding of mirrors. Central to the story is that the hero will turn to stone if he looks at Medusa, and is saved by using a reflection.

Other visual concepts are more easily addressed. A Year 1 child with low vision has never seen footprints and is confused by a story about a dog making muddy footmarks. Her understanding is increased when she is able to make and feel footprints in the sand.

Shared writing

Shared reading and writing are whole-class activities that should be interlinked and highly interactive. In shared writing the teacher acts as a scribe to record the class idea and demonstrates specific writing skills – ranging from how to form a letter, to planning and drafting a story. Shared writing is also used to focus on spelling, grammar, punctuation and handwriting. In taking a supportive role, the teacher enables children to work at a level beyond their independent writing skills.

Because the writing develops from ideas given by the class it is not possible to provide the text in Braille or large print in advance. This means that if children have no access to what is being presented to the class they require an extra adult to scribe what the class teacher is writing.

Adaptations need to reflect the needs of individual children. To increase the general accessibility to the text, class teachers can use good quality pens, bigger font size and leave enough space between lines so that they can edit the text without it getting too cluttered. Using different colours may help children locate parts of the text that have been edited.

Some children with low vision may require an extra adult to provide them with their own copy of the text in large bold font. They may need help to find specific parts of the text or demonstrations to be given in close view. These children may require time outside the Literacy Hour to consolidate aspects learnt, for example how to form a letter.

To adapt shared writing sessions for children with no vision is a harder challenge. Some sessions may be inappropriate, for example discussing the shape of a letter in print. It may be more effective to withdraw the child and work on the corresponding Braille skills. These children need the support of an extra adult who scribes what is being presented to the class in a Braille format.

The Braille code consists of a combination of six dots per cell. Each cell can represent a letter or a group of letters, i.e. because Braille is very exact in terms of letter/contractions shapes and spacing, it is not very easy to edit a text in Braille. For example, you cannot simply erase a full stop, put it somewhere else and still keep the correct spacing between words. It may help if as much of the text as possible can be prepared in advance. For example, making several cards with magnetic strips with words and punctuation that are likely to be part of the text. These could then be put on a metal tray and moved around as necessary. However, this does not avoid the need for producing some cards on the spot. This method is impractical when working on a long text. It would be more effective to scribe the Braille and introduce changes by using cards with magnetic strips or blu-tack.

If the session is based on a piece of writing completed by a child the day before, then it should be written in Braille before the Literacy Hour. In this case, there could be double space between lines of Braille, and cards with magnetic strips with possible words or punctuation used to substitute the ones given in the text.

Word and Sentence Level

Word and sentence level work involves the teaching of phonics, spelling, vocabulary, grammar and punctuation. The access issues are similar to those addressed in the section on shared reading and writing.

However, there are some specific issues for Braille users regarding the teaching of spelling. As a verbal activity the teaching of spelling for Braille or print is the same. As a written activity, it is different. For example, teachers often call children's attention to common letter strings in words. In Braille there are contractions and these letter strings may vary. For example, 'ou' words include those using the contraction for 'ou', 'ound', 'ount', 'ought', 'through' and short forms of 'although', 'could', 'should', etc. In this situation, it will be more effective to provide individual teaching on Braille writing.

Guided reading

In guided reading children have their own copy of the same book and read with the support of the teacher in small ability banded groups. The text is unknown and they are encouraged to apply new and learnt reading skills to extract meaning and form their own opinions of the passage.

Planning for individual children

The Braille user. Braille is decoded through touch and each cell has to be read sequentially cell by cell. Braille users cannot therefore skim and scan text or take advantage of the visual patterns of words. The knowledge of frequently used words will not be aided by recognising visual shapes. The code contains nearly 200 short forms or contractions and studies indicate that Braille is significantly slower to read than print. Braille is made up of individual letters so a dot in the wrong place completely changes the meaning, making it impossible for an adult who is not a Braille user to access why a child has made an error.

A child who is learning to read Braille will need to learn additional reading skills on a regular basis. Traditionally the teaching of Braille has been skills based. These methods can be used as an argument for excluding children from guided reading sessions but there is little research on this and much will depend on the individual child.

The print user. Unlike the Braille reader, a child with low vision who uses print will be able to take advantage of the decoding skills that are being taught to the group. Although it is possible to skim and scan enlarged print, that task is more difficult and more tiring. It is also more difficult to recognise letter patterns when the print is large. Again, it is likely that they will be disadvantaged by the speed they are able to process the information.

Children in a mainstream class with impaired vision may take longer to become fluent readers that their peers. This in itself should not influence their grouping by ability. Understanding, expressive language and response to literature should all be considered.

Materials. Books need to be reproduced in the appropriate code and format. Page numbers will need to correspond to the other children's book so it is possible for them to locate the same passages. This will not be possible with a longer text as the Braille or large print will occupy more pages than the print copy and the clas teacher needs to be aware of the corresponding pages.

Where there is a reliance on pictures to understand the context, real object or additional explanations will need to be substituted. If a child uses a CCTV for reading it will be important to physically accommodate the equipment so the child remains within the group.

Guided writing

Guided writing is a group activity with intensive support from the teacher. These sessions aim to teach children to write independently and often flow from the shared writing work.

Children with vision impairment benefit from input on some specific aspects of the writing process such as planning a piece of writing, expanding or contracting a text, constructing complex sentences and checking for grammatical agreement. However, there are some differences for these children.

Planning for individual children

The Braille user. As for reading, there are differences between writing in print and in Braille. Braille users cannot write and check their writing at the same time and editing a text in Braille is much more laborious that in print. These children need extra time to complete tasks and the support of an adult with Braille skills who can understand the child's writing.

It is also important for Braille users to have access to their peers' work both by listening to what they have written or by having a Braille copy of their text.

The print user. A print user benefits from the teaching and modelling of the writing process. These children will require extra time, however, as some tasks are more laborious – for example proof reading, editing and using a dictionary. This work needs to be extended beyond the hour to include for example handwriting and touch typing skills.

Materials. Braille users may use a laptop with speech or a Brailler with a printer attached. Print users may benefit from using dark lined paper and bold pencil or black felt pen or a laptop.

Independent activities

Children are expected to work on their own or with other children for 20 minutes during the hour to develop independent reading and writing strategies. The work can be linked to the shared activities or can be separate tasks.

Planning for individual children

It may be necessary to use one or two of the 'independent' sessions a week to concentrate on the different aspects of reading and writing that children with impaired vision have to learn. During the remaining three sessions a week the child would be able to join the class group, e.g. a guided group and/or cooperative work with another child and/or independent work.

Procedures. Developing independence is more difficult for a child with impaired vision and they need to be provided with precise instructions and have access to adapted planning boards, for example where each activity is represented with a tactile symbol.

Locating objects and people have to be formally learnt and strategies developed for when procedures go wrong. In classrooms, equipment and furniture are inevitably moved around or put in the wrong place and it would be possible for a child to spend the whole sessions locating equipment. A boy who was partially sighted and an excellent reader was observed finding his piece of work, one of thirty. This exercise took him over five minutes because just locating and reading each name was slow and labourious.

Materials. The extent to which a child with impaired vision can take part will depend on the presentation of the activity and what they are required to do. Many interesting activities that engage children are highly dependent on visual skills and will require adaptation for visually impaired children. They include cutting and pasting, highlighting words, investigations that include references to a range of books, dictionary work, speech bubbles, word searches, colour coding, bullet points and flow charts.

Activities for all. When children are required to work cooperatively the activity needs to be designed so all children can contribute on an equal basis. Activities can be changed. So, for example, rather than locating and highlighting all the verbs on a page, the answers could be recorded onto tape by the group. Cards in both Braille and print could be provided for a cloze procedure.

Activities to be modified. Some objectives lend themselves to activities where children work on their own. These activities can be modified so that the activity is different but the learning outcome is the same. For example, where children are required to investigate labels around the school, a modified activity might consist of providing a tactile map of the school with the Braille labels included. This map could be produced on a concept keyboard with sound clues. It would also be necessary to provide some Braille labels around the school to consolidate this work. Where sighted children have pictures and labels to match, an alternative might be real objects or a tactile diagram and labels.

Role of the support teacher/LSA. This role will vary depending how much support is needed for each activity. For example, when a child is being expected to work independently the support will have to be directed to preparation so the activity can be undertaken independently. Other activities will require the support of an adult, for example when investigating back cover blurbs in the school library or when children are required to check each others' work.

Plenary

Children with vision impairment will have limited access to what other children are showing during the plenary session. Children with some vision should sit where the demonstrations are accessible to them. All children with vision impairment benefit from extra verbal input and whenever possible it is important for them to touch, have a Braille copy or to have a close look at the work being discussed.

12 Children with autistic spectrum disorder

Frances Brook and Heather Clewley

This chapter is about children with autistic spectrum disorder. It describes some of the difficulties they are likely to meet during the Literacy Hour, and particular strategies which will make sure they can be fully included.

Introduction

Many children with autistic spectrum disorder (ASD) thrive in the Literacy Hour. The element of routine and predictability gives a structure to their day, particularly necessary for those who find it hard to cope with change. They may do very well in mastering high frequency words, phonic patterns, grammatical and spelling rules; public success in the shared word and sentence level work section of the hour can be a welcome experience, and boost their image of themselves as learners. It will be important for the teacher to remember, however, that apparently good word and sentence level skills can mask real difficulties in understanding at text level; grasping the nuances of text, particularly where these relate to social understandings of how people think, feel and behave, is likely to prove very difficult for them. So too will the social framework of working with other children in the group work section of the hour.

Shared Reading and Writing

The child with ASD may have difficulties in the following areas during the shared part of the Literacy Hour.

Sitting on the carpet

- because of being in close proximity with group
- because of sensory difficulties
- because of not understanding what is happening
- because of poor body posture/fidgeting.

Demonstrating attention to speaker

- little or no eye contact
- not raising hand to respond to questions
- sitting with back to the teacher.

Attending to speech

- because of distractions in environment
- problems with processing language
- poor auditory memory
- not understanding language or knowing how it works.

Social understanding

- not perceiving selves as part of the group
- not automatically copying what the group are doing
- copying what the group are doing but not understanding why
- taking on inappropriate roles (e.g. teacher/LSA)
- appearing arrogant and pedantic
- wanting to have their own way
- continually asking questions or interrupting
- not being able to pick out the significant features of a social situation
- not being able to pick up on non-verbal cues to transfer attention from teacher to the book/blackboard.

Organisational skills

- of themselves and their equipment.

Gaining attention

- repeated interruptions
- continual questioning
- standing up and walking 'through' the group to get to the teacher.

Answering abstract questions

- 'What did you do to work out this word?'

Moving from the shared time to independent and group work

- because of the problems of coping with change.

The following suggested strategies are not necessarily the right answer for every child with ASD. A key principle for staff is to try to analyse what the presenting behaviour is saying about the child's difficulties in that specific situation.

The most successful outcomes are gained from gaining knowledge of the child. A basic understanding of autism is essential for staff involved with teaching these children. Nevertheless, it may well be worth trying some of the following.

- Share in advance with child the specific objective of lesson/activity, so they see the point of what they have to do.
- Seat the child beside the LSA who can act as a 'role model' and quietly provide appropriate verbal and physical prompts.
- Use a little version of the 'Big Book' with the child during group time. The LSA can prompt the child's attention to the appropriate sentence or picture. (This is not usually advocated but may be necessary if the child is to be part of the session.)
- Use a line drawing, cross or photograph of the child to indicate where he or she will sit on the carpet for the group work – it may be that the child needs to sit at the edge of the group because of problems with close proximity.
- Provide a small table and chair situated to the side of the group if necessary – even if the rest of the group is sitting on the carpet. The child can see the appropriate behaviour of the rest of the class.
- Use the child's name first if you specifically want him to respond.
- Appropriate ways of gaining attention will need to be taught and practised in one to one sessions with the LSA, then used as targets in the Literacy Hour sessions. It is important to acknowledge verbally when the child has responded appropriately.
- Obsessions can be used as motivators/rewards.
- Use a visual timetable to show the child that there will be changes during the session. Pre-tutoring and practise may be needed in advance.

- Use of 'social scripts' to teach appropriate social skills and routines.
- For the teacher and support staff to use non-verbal cues to augment their speech (e.g. index fingers touch corners of eyes – 'look'; hand cups ear – 'listen'; finger to lips – 'quiet').
- Explain text language that the child might take literally (metaphor, simile, sarcasm) – like the phrase 'raining cats and dogs'.

Whole-class Word and Sentence Level Work

Although this part of the hour may be relatively accessible for the child with ASD, it is important to be aware of potential pitfalls. For example, the child's reading ability is likely to be above his or her level of understanding, so that particular attention will need to be paid to explaining and teaching the meaning of vocabulary. The child will often display the 'knows it one day – but not the next' syndrome, so repetition and patience will be needed. Suggested strategies include:

- Differentiating and individualising work content, and presenting it in a structured manner (translated and broken down into simple steps).
- Presenting the work in a simple and well-spaced format, with clear 'start' and 'stop' signs.
- Using 'Cloze' procedures – writing out the sentence, leaving the child to complete one or two words.
- Differentiating questions and tasks to match the child's understanding and ability.
- Thinking of ways to involve the child at the social level if the content of the teaching is beyond their grasp (e.g. choosing the children with hands up to answer questions, being responsible for handing out materials, cleaning the whiteboard).
- Making a conscious effort to acknowledge and include the child with ASD as much as the others.

Guided Reading and Writing

This phase of the hour can present particular difficulties to the child with ASD – for example, in trying to predict events in stories or discuss how the characters are thinking or feeling. Problems will relate to :

- understanding meaning
- understanding sequencing of events and pictures
- understanding the difference between various genres – between an instruction and a poem, for example
- defining fact and fiction
- using intonation when reading
- understanding another person's point of view
- understanding hypothetical situations (e.g. 'pretend you are an angry shopkeeper')
- generalising knowledge
- understanding and interpreting pun, joke, metaphor, etc.
- appreciating different communicative purposes.

Helpful strategies include:

- Explaining any abstract and difficult content: for example, 'The Paper Boy' – a story where the child with ASD assumed the boy was made of paper.
- Providing visual prompts to show what is expected (e.g. using line drawings to reinforce where to listen, talk, write, or start/stop work can be more meaningful than a verbal prompt).

- Checking that the child knows how sequences are indicated (e.g. a, b, c/1, 2, 3).
- Checking that the child has understanding of the basic concepts used such as 'before', 'after', etc.
- Using non-fiction and photographs or symbols wherever possible, since these are concrete and will help the child's understanding.
- Encouraging the child to imitate his or her peers (those demonstrating appropriate behaviours!).
- Being aware of the child's likely difficulty in understanding another's point of view.

Independent activities

This session of the Literacy Hour will often be the easiest part for the children with ASD, when they will feel most comfortable socially and with regard to understanding what work they have to do. Nevertheless, there can be problems. The teacher's expectations of the child being able to complete work independently may be too high. Going back over and repeating work can seem pointless to the child – 'once work is done, it's done'. He or she may also have problems with committing anything to paper because of poor fine motor skills, the change of activity, sensory difficulties, being able to start and stop and making mistakes. It will help if you:

- Provide a set place to work in a distraction free environment – sometimes in a separate work base a little aside from other children.
- Pre-tutor and rehearse work styles (e.g. reading in unison, silent reading, turntaking when reading with a partner).
- Use any specific obsessions or interests the child may have to motivate or complete work.
- Use clear 'starts' and 'finishes' – schedules, timers, clocks, traffic lights all provide concrete, visual structure.
- Teach appropriate work skills (e.g. left to right, top to bottom – use line drawings (PCS) and symbols on an 'order of work strip' to give visual reinforcement).
- Plan small amount of work and targets to engender success at completing work (building self-confidence and self-esteem).
- Make activities practical – the more practical the better.
- Make use of 'writing frames'.
- To combat fine motor or sensory difficulties, be prepared to allow the child to use a laptop, word processor, rubber stamps, or audiotape to record work.
- Try to incorporate a multi-sensory approach.
- Plan a gradual progression throughout the week from one to one teaching to small group work and then to independent work using a single theme.

Plenary

Most of the previously listed 'anticipated difficulties' will be applicable to this session, particularly as it is for such a short time. However, it is important to include the child with ASD in this session as it emphasises 'the finish' of literacy hour. Suggested strategies might be:

- Giving the child with ASD responsibility (e.g. as 'time keeper' to say when it is time for the plenary session to begin).
- Using prompt and question cards.
- Since children with ASD have particular difficulty with understanding their own personal involvement with past events, using this session to work on recall and memory.
- Letting the child have his or her own piece of work to talk about – use an object of reference or a prompt card as a visual reinforcer for the child.

Section 4

Using Information and Communication Technology in the Literacy Hour

13 Using Information and Communication Technology

Linda Johnson and Ayleen Driver

This section highlights opportunities to use ICT in the Literacy Hour.

Pupils with learning difficulties benefit particularly from being able to use ICT to reinforce their learning. In addition, we have cross referenced linked ICT activities for Literacy with the QCA Exemplar Scheme of Work for ICT to show how including ICT in the Literacy Hour can meet the objectives of the National Curriculum.

There are few specific references to the use of ICT in the Framework for Teaching the National Literacy Strategy, yet there are many literacy activities which could be enhanced, and certainly made more exciting for pupils, by the use of ICT. Many of the activities are suitable for all pupils, not just those with special educational needs. Pupils with special needs often have high order ICT skills and they can be encouraged in age-appropriate ICT activities.

Introduction

The activities suggested in this chapter are not all-encompassing with regard to the ICT Programmes of Study, but are a taster for the ways in which ICT may be integrated into teaching and learning as far as literacy is concerned.

The Communicating Strand for ICT and developing literacy are inextricably linked – whenever children write, they could do so using a word processor or desktop publishing package. A computer in the classroom is a great resource for both independent, group and class work and is too valuable a tool to remain unused during the development of literacy skills. It remains a great motivator and encourages collaborative work that can become more focused as children's attention is extended.

Not to be forgotten is the computer as a great tool for making teaching resources, especially in the production of 'texts'. A4 size printouts can easily be enlarged to A3 on the school photocopier. CD-ROM and the Internet can be a wonderful source of texts.

We would recommend that an ICT toolbox to support the development of literacy skills includes:

- A tape recorder/playback (multi user headphones) – teach the pupils how to rewind for you!
- Franklin Spellcheckers – not just for the spelling lists, but for the games too.
- A computer with colour printout, and hopefully sound.
- A good word processor. The more features it has, the better.
  e.g. Can it run at different levels for different ages and abilities?
       Can it 'talk'?
       Does it 'spellcheck'? – check for grammar?
       Does it have 'on screen help' – wordbanks?
       Can it pull in pictures?

- A text decoding program.
- A wordpuzzle program.
- A spelling program.
- CD-ROM and Internet access – reading for information, E-mail.
- DTP package.
- A database.
- Talking books.

Selection of useful software

A selection of suggested software follows but is not exclusive and will be ever changing as new packages are developed.

Word processors

Talking Write Away (Blackcat)
Clicker Plus (Crick)
I Can Write (Resource)

Text decoding

WinTray (REM)

Spelling and Punctuation

Talking Animated Alphabet (Sherston)
My First Incredible Amazing Dictionary (Dorling Kindersley)
Word Shark 2 (REM)
Starspell (REM)
Speaking
Sherlock (Topologica)

Word puzzles

Wordsearch (Inclusive Technology)

Talking Books

Ridiculous Rhymes (Sherston)
Rusty Dreamer (Sherston)
Matti Moles Summer Holiday (Sherston)
Oxford Reading Tree Talking Stories
Max and the Machines (Flying Boot)
Tortoise and the Hare
Grandma and Me
New Kids on the Block

CD-ROM

Kingfisher Micropaedia (REM)
Encarta (Microsoft)
Ancient Lands (Microsoft)
Compton's Multimedia Encyclopaedia
Any Dorling Kindersley package

A variety of useful CD-ROM resources are also available to support some of the widely used reading schemes such as Fuzzbuzz, Oxford Reading Tree, Wellington Square.

DTP

Textease (REM)

Databases

Information Workshop (Blackcat)
Numberbox (Blackcat)
Tree (REM)

IT in the Literacy Hour

To use the activities in this section:
1.   Find the correct Year group
2.   Identify the learning objective in the NLS in the first three columns
3.   Consider the activities which support that target.

Literacy Strategy Learning Objectives			Suggested IT Activities Linked to NLS **Year: Reception**	QCA IT Scheme of Work
Page No	Term	Objective	Unit	
18		W1	Use CD-ROM and other interactive resources which illustrate rhyme. Using a word processor and a prepared rhyme with some rhyming words missing, but available on screen or via a concept keyboard, work with the class/group to select and complete the rhymes.	1C
18		W3	Use CD-ROM and other interactive programs to learn alaphabet and letter sounds.	1C
18		S1	Click and listen to a variety of sentences, some coherent, some not, constructed on a talking word processor. Write and listen to a sentence using a talking word processor with word selections on screen or a concept keyboard (also page 19, Text Level Work, Item 11 – Writing)	1A
18		T1, 12	Use a program that matches pictures to words and can join them into sentences.	1A
19		T12	Write names/labels on pictures created in an art package which incorporates text.	1A
19		T15	Use a simple word processor to create lists, labels, etc.	1A

Literacy Strategy Learning Objectives			Suggested IT Activities Linked to NLS **Year: One**	QCA IT Scheme of Work
Page No	Term	Objective		Unit
20	1	W2	Use similar program to reinforce rhyme. If already used at Reception, set to more sophisticated level in menu.	1C
20	1 (also 2 and 3)	W7 (4, 2)	Use Talking Storybook Versions available for some reading schemes (e.g. Oxford Reading Tree).	1C
20	1 (also 2 and 3)	S2	Shared activity using prepared text with missing words (possibly rhyming) which acn be inserted from on screen selection. (This activity also appropriate for Text Level Work, Item 2).	1B
20	1 (also 2)	S8 (5)	Pupils to insert full stops into created texts – sentences,some more than a line long. Leave a line space between sentences when creating text, so that pupils need simply Insert a full stop on the end of each sentence.	1A
20	1	T9, 11	Could use any word processor for this suggested Literacy activity.	1A
20	1	T14–16	As above, including graphics package.	1B
22	2	T3	Use Talking Books.	1C
23	2	T13	Complete prepared text using a selection of rhyming words from on screen display or concept keyboard.	1B
23	2	T22–25	Could use any word processor for this suggested Literacy activity.	1B
24	3	S7	Add question marks to a selection of prepared sentences. Leave a line space between sentences when creating text, so that pupils need simply insert a question mark on the end of each sentence.	1A
24	3	T11	Create the class poem using a word processor.	1B
24	3	T13, 14, 16	Could use any word processor for these suggested Literacy activities.	1B
25	3	T15	Use a prepared text on word processor, to be edited as described in Literacy Strategy manual.	1B
25	3	T20–22	Could use any word processor for these suggested Literacy activities.	1B

Literacy Strategy Learning Objectives			Suggested IT Activities Linked to NLS **Year: Two**	QCA IT Scheme of Work
Page No	Term	Objective		Unit
26 (28)	1 (also 2)	S4 S(3)	Use a word processor to create and print own writing, then edit for sense and punctuation and print again. (Both copies may be used for assesment purposes.)	2A
26	1	S5	Edit a prepared text to insert capitals for names where required. (Original text shows lower case ready to be suBstituted.)	2A
26	1	S6	Use CD-ROM resources to illustrate how ideas and information can be linked organisationally through use of arrows and boxes.	2C
26–27	1	T9–12 15	Can use any word processor, preferably one with a spellchecker, for these writing tasks. Some 'scaffolding' may be provided via a prepared text to be extended by the pupil.	2A
28	2	S6, 7	Provide a set of pictures with empty speech bubbles. Discuss how speech bubbles can be used to illustrate direct speech. Remind the class how to enter text and demonstrate the use of shift key. Working in pairs, pupils to use word processor to type speech, print and stick into bubbles. Experiment with font sizes and syles for a variety of speech bubbles.	2A
28 (30)	2 (also 3)	S8 S(4)	Create prepared lists along the line in a word processor without commas. Pupils to insert commas and print. (May like to illustrate for presentation.)	2A
28	2	S9	Can use any word processor for this task.	2A
28	2	T6	Create scaffolded character descriptions in a word processor with selection of describing words available either on screen or via concept keyboard. Pupils to enhance the description using text help available and their own ideas.	2A
28	2	T9	Use CD-ROM resources which illustrate patterns of rhyme, rhyme and other features of sound in different poems.	2C
29	2	T15	Create and save a prepared poem for pupils to extend or substitute elements, inventing own lines, verses.	2A
29	2	T16–19	Make use of electronic spellmasters and CD-ROM reference resources to illustrate the use of indexing, glossaries and diagrams.	2C
29	2	T20	Can use any word processor for this task.	2A

Literacy Strategy Learning Objectives			Suggested IT Activities Linked to NLS **Year: Two**	QCA IT Scheme of Work
Page No	Term	Objective		Unit
30	3	S2	Using a word processor, create and save a prepared text in which the verbs do not agree with the nouns/ pronouns. Ask pupils to correct and print.	2A
30	3	S5	Can use any word processor for this task.	2A
30	3	S6	Using a word processor, create and save a series of statements which can be turned into questions by substituting from a range of 'wh' words – who, what, where – possibly available on screen or from a concept keyboard, and adding a question mark. Pupils to print their work.	2A
30–31	3	T9–12, 14, 19–21	Could use any word processor for these suggested Literacy activities. Some 'scaffolding' (i.e. partly prepared texts may be helpful).	2A
31	3	T15–17	Use CD-ROM reference resources which have contents and index, highlighted key words, etc.	2C

Literacy Strategy Learning Objectives			Suggested IT Activities Linked to NLS **Year: Three**	QCA IT Scheme of Work
Page No	Term	Objective		Unit
32	1	S3	Using a word processor create and save a series of sentences with their verbs missing. Pupils to insert appropriate verbs (possibly available as a selection on screen), in a style or colour which makes it stand out in its sentence.	3A
			As above, but this time the verbs are there waiting to be substituted by others through the use of overtyping and of Search/Replace technique.	3A/4A
32	1	S4	Create and save a 'present' tense text using a word processor. Ask the pupil to change it to the past tense by overtyping the verbs (which may be highlighted). Print work.	3A
32	1	S7	Working in pairs, pupils to write a short dialogue making use of SHIFT/speech mark keys. Print.	
			Using a prepared text that has only closing speech marks and no capital letters, pupils to insert opening speech marks (position highlighted with an X) and capitals to mark the start of direct speech. Print.	3A
33	1	S9	Pupils to create slogans, messages, titles which include a variety of fonts, styles, including italics used for effect.	3A
33	1	S10–13	Create and save a perpared text which then requires pupils to undertake the revision and consolidation of skills from KS1 – missing punctuation, including commas, and some missing verbs. Pupils to review through editing and print.	2A/3A
32	1	T11	Create a prepared text which describes a known place in outline (i.e. a scaffolded text, that pupils are to complete using their own adjectives or ones provided as a selection on screen/from a concept keyboard/from a card). Merge this text with a picture.	3A
33 (34)	1 (also 2)	T12 (2)	As with a class poem, get pupils to brainstorm adjectives *onto* a joint 'themed' page (e.g. words that describe smell, colour, movement). Make a collection of pages, each with its own 'logo' and print to make a class book.	3A
33	1	T15	Create a prepared compacted text, possibly topic related. Pupils to reorganise the text into paragraphs and merge in a picture.	3A
33	1	T19, 20	Make use of reference type CD-ROM resources.	3A
33	1	T21, 22	Make the link to ideas of key words, gathering information from more than one source, organising and presenting, by using a database. Make notes using a word processor.	3C

Literacy Strategy Learning Objectives			Suggested IT Activities Linked to NLS **Year: Three**	QCA IT Scheme of Work
Page No	Term	Objective		Unit
35	2	W24	Pupils to edit a prepared text so that it becomes 'the opposite' of the original (i.e. all words which have an opposite are changed). (The tall/short girl was very happy/sad to win/lose the competition.)	
34 (36)	2 (also 3)	S (S)1 (1)	Use a text decoding program which enables the teacher to create a passage and hide all or part of it. Pupils then have to gradually 'expose' it by predicting letters/words, thus making use of their awareness of grammer, spelling, context clues, etc.	
2	34	S2	In pairs pupils edit a prepared passage in which the only adjective used (several times) is the word 'nice'. They must change each one to a different, more appropriate choice. Some help may be given, if desired, by a selection of alternatives available either on screen or on a card. Print and save. Pairs call up someone else's saved text from above and change the adjectives yet again.	
34	2	S4	Pupils to change 'singular' style passage into a 'plural' one and/or vice versa. Print. This could be a 'round Robin' exercise with the whole class.	
35	2	S9	Working in pairs, pupils to delete a given number of words from a prepared text so that it still makes sense. Print.	
34–35	2	T6–11 16, 17	All of these suggested NLS activities can be undertaken using a word processor. The specific IT skills of using alignment for layout – justifying left, right and centre – can be used in items 8 – writing a letter; and 12, writing, rules, recipes, lists, etc.	3E if then sent on E-mail
35	2	T13	NLS makes specific reference to instructional texts including IT. This could involve an evaluation of program notes, help cards, instructions for the use of peripherals such as Roamers, spellmasters. Pupils might write evaluations of the on screen instructions that appear in various packages.	
37	3	W11	Create and save a prepared text for pupils to edit so that words become contracted by deleting and using an apostrophe (e.g. could not = couldn't). Print.	
36–37	3	T10–15 17–26	All of these NLS activities can be undertaken by using a word processor. (Note: 17 and 21 state clearly that IT should be used!) Suggest for 13: Create and save a half screen story to be extended by pupils working in pairs. Each pair to print 3 copies of their version (one each and one for teacher). Suggest for 22: Use a DTP package for writing the news report.	3E if any text sent via E-mail

Literacy Strategy Learning Objectives			Suggested IT Activities Linked to NLS **Year: Four**	QCA IT Scheme of Work
Page No	Term	Objective		Unit
38	1	W6	Create a prepared text, substituting an 'x' or star for a number of common homophones (e.g. to/too/two). Ask pupils to insert the missing words and to highlight them in bold typeface. They should then print their work and return the screen to its original state (by either reversing editing processes or by calling up the original file).	4A
39	1	W13	Look at the way newspapers and magazines display advertising slogans and headlines. Use a variety of fonts and effects to present your own rhyming jingle. Print.	4A
38	1	S2	Create a prepared text in a past, present or future tense about a male/female character. Ask pupils to edit so that the tense and gender are changed, making use of search and replace techniques for some of the changes. Print.	4A
38	1	S Combine 3 and 5	Create a prepared text which is lacking in imaginative verbs and commas to make grammatical boundaries within sentences. Include some spelling mistakes. Pupils should edit to produce a more sophisticated text, making use of a spellcheck if required. Print.	4A
38–39	1	T9–14, 15	Any word processor could be used for these activities. Create a prepared condensed text which is incorrectly sequenced. Firstly pupils make a printout. Then using cut and paste techniques they should reorganise the text into sequenced paragraphs and print. They can return screen to original state by reversing operations or calling up original file.	4A
39	1	T23	Specific reference is made to the use of IT texts here. CD-ROMs for information finding would be most appropriate.	
39	1	T24–27	Word processors could be used for any of these activities, but for item 24 a DTP program would be most appropriate.	4A
41	2	W9	Create a prepared text littered with common choice words (e.g. got, nice, good, then) and ask pupils to edit (using search and replace techniques) so that more imaginative choices improve the text. Pupils to print and return screen to original state.	4A
41	2	W10	As above, but using search and replace to make gender changes to a text. Further editing may be required due to this gender change!	4A

Literacy Strategy Learning Objectives			Suggested IT Activities Linked to NLS **Year: Four**	QCA IT Scheme of Work
Page No	Term	Objective		Unit
40	2	S2	Ask pupils to insert commas into a prepared text and then print. The text could also include some spelling mistakes (highlighted) necessitating the use of a spellcheck.	4A
41	2	S4	Create a prepared text comprising pairs of sentences which pupils can join by editing in connectives and commas. Print.	
40–41	2	T10–14	You can use any word processor for these activities.	4A
41	2	T17	CD-ROM information programs particularly useful here.	
41	2	T18	Make use of a word processor and different font, or style (e.g. underlining) to mark extracts.	4A
41	2	T21–25	Use a word processor for any of these activities.	4A
42	3	S3	Create a series of prepared texts to be edited by pupils so that statements become questions, questions become orders, etc.	4A
42	3	T8	Create a 'scaffolded' text, maybe paragraph starts, for this challenging activity. Pupils may then make use of the spellcheck and possibly use search/replace, cut and paste.	4A
42	3	T11–15	Can use a word processor for any of these but especially Activity 15– it's ideal!	4A
42	3	T20–25	Can use a word processor for any of these but *especially* Activity 24 – the paragraph could be a prepared text to be slimmed down. Activity 25 – use a DTP package or a 'Works' program or a combined art/text program.	4A 4A possibly 4B

Literacy Strategy Learning Objectives			Suggested IT Activities Linked to NLS **Year: Five**	QCA IT Scheme of Work
Page No	Term	Objective		Unit
45	1	W10	Using a word processor, create and save a prepared dialogue for pupils to extend by editing and inserting adverbs to qualify verbs. If the word processor used has a thesaurus, pupils should make use of this. They should print them and return screen to original display.	
44	1	S1	Create and save a prepared text for pupils to manipulate – deleting and re-arranging words without damaging the basic meaning.	
44	1	S4	Create and save a prepared poster advertising an event/a newsletter/an appeal. Ask pupils to edit it for a variety of different readers (e.g. younger children, adults, teenagers). Ensure that some graphics are available for manipulation as well as text.	5A
44	1	S5	Provide a prepared text which uses direct speech and ask pupils to edit it into reported speech (an/or vice versa).	
45	1	T13, 15–18, 24–26	All of these activities can be undertaken using a word processor.	
45	2	S1	Create and save a prepared text of simple sentences. Ask pupils to re-order them, making use of editing facilities available within the word processor, after which they would print their version and restore the original text on screen.	
45	2	S3	Create and save a story introduction, possibly with some graphics. The task for pupils is to 'customise' this story start for a different audience – older, younger, to appeal to lovers of horror stories, animal stories, etc. Then print and restore original text to screen.	5A if graphics used
47	2	S8 and 9	Create a series of saved texts to be used by pupils for consolidating skills such as combining two or more sentences by using connectives or commas, etc. They print their edited version then return the original text to screen.	
46–47	2	T11–13, 21–22	All of these writing activities can be undertaken using a word processor.	
47	2	T17	Specific reference is made in the NLS Framework to the use of CD-ROM and other IT information resources for this item.	

Literacy Strategy Learning Objectives			Suggested IT Activities linked to NLS: **Year Five**	QCA IT Scheme of Work
Page No	Term	Objective		Unit

48	3	S3	Create and save prepared text containing a significant number of prepositions and ask the pupils to:
			
			   – highlight them in some way and make a printout;
			
			then
			
			    – substitute other prepositions in their place, making any other edits required as a result.
			
			Produce a second printout then return the text to its original state.	

48	3	S4	Create and save a prepared text comprising some complex sentences but missing punctuations for pupils to punctuate, then print. They should finally return the original to screen (by calling up file name).	
48	3		Create a prepared text which can then be extended and developed by pupils through linking clauses and sentences together.	
48	3	T7, 9–11 17–19	All these activities can be undertaken using a word processor and graphics if illustrations are appropriate. In Activity 17, reference is made to writing a news editorial or a leaflet so a DTP package may be helpful.	Possibly 5A if graphics used

Literacy Strategy Learning Objectives			Suggested IT Activities Linked to NLS **Year: Six**	QCA IT Scheme of Work
Page No	Term	Objective		Unit
50	1	S2	Using a word processor or DTP package, prepare a saved text in active form and ask pupils to edit it, to read in passive form, or vice versa. They should print their version and then return the original text to screen.	
50–51	1	T6–10, 14–18	All of these activities can be undertaken using a word processor. Item 18 makes specific reference to the use of IT for the activity. Items 14 and 18 could be facilitated through a DTP package. Some texts created here by pupils may become pages for use on the Internet, or as part of a multimedia presentation.	6A if Internet or multi-media used
52	2	S1, 3, 4	As described for earlier years, prepared texts may be created ready for pupils to edit and extend through punctuating, changing tense, contracting, substituting, etc. They should print their version, then return the original text to screen.	
53	2	T10–14, 18, 19	A word processor may be used for any of these activities.	
54	3	S4	Pupils may use editing features in a word processor, such as cut and paste techniques, to explore different versions of a prepared text through the manipulation of clauses.	
44–55	3	T8–10, 13, 14, 20, 21	All of these activities can be undertaken using a word processor. Some may become pages for the Internet or part of a multimedia presentation.	6A if Internet or multi-media used

Index

Active Learning Activities 14–15
adults 15, 18, 46, 82 *see also* Learning Support
    Assistant; support staff
age appropriateness 30
attention 9–10
autistic spectrum disorder, children with 70,
    87–90

behaviour 9–10 *see also* behaviour difficulties
behaviour difficulties 34–44 *see also* EBD
behaviour rating sheet 42, **44**
Braille 82, 83, 84–5, 86
British Sign Language (BSL) 80

CD-ROM 33, 93
'catch up' programmes 19–22 *see also*
    Oxfordshire: Catch Up programme
children
    role of 8–9
    taking responsibility for behaviour 38–9
choices 39
class teacher 7, 9–12, 82
Cloze 15, 89
coding systems 15
communication difficulties 70–77
contributing 10

DISTAR 21
DTP software 94
databases 94
differentiation 7, 12, 13–18, 46–52, **73**, 76, 77, **77**
Down's Syndrome 46
dyslexia 5, 13, 70
dyspraxia 70

EBD 5, 46, 70
    managing 34–44
enlarged print 82, 85

Family Literacy 4, 19, 20
feedback 12
fiction 14, 16, **17**
five day/five step programme 23–9

global learning difficulties 53–68
group and independent time *see* independent
    and group time
group reading resources **33**
guided reading 10–11, 25–6, **32**, 47, **65**, **68**, 75, 79,
    80, 84–5, 89–90
guided writing **65**, **68**, 80, 85, 89–90

hearing losses, children with 46, 70, 78–80
high frequency words 6, **6**, 7, 26, **28**, **29**, 61–3

independence and self-esteem, resources for **33**
independent and group time
    and autistic spectrum disorder 90
    and behaviour difficulties 35, **35**, 38, 40–41
    and complex needs class **65**, **68**
    and differentiation 13–18, 47, 49
    as element of literacy hour 3
    and 'out of step' children **31**, **32**
    and SEN 4, 11–12, 27, **28**
    and speech and language difficulties 76, **77**
    using structured programmes in 19–22
    and vision impairment 85–6
Individual Education Plans (IEPs) 3, 4, 6, 7, 8,
    15, 18, 24, 35, 41–2, 43, 71
individual management plan 35
information and communication technology
    (ICT) 6, **33**, 82, 92–104
input, differentiation by 15
instructional reading **33**
instructions 38

Key Stage 1   20, 23, 30, 37, 54, **63**, **64**, **65**, **66**, **67**,
    68
Key Stage 2   5, 14, 15, 21, 23

Launch into Reading Success 20
Learning Support Assistant (LSA) 5, 7, 8, 11, 18,
    20, 39, 46, 49, 82, 86, 88
letter writing 49, **50**, **51**
light source 78
listening 9
literacy difficulties 5

matching 15
moderate learning difficulties 70
multi-sensory activities 25, **25**, 26

National Curriculum 92
National Literacy Strategy/Fra
    22, 23–4, 36, 92, 94–104
noise sources 78
non-fiction 14

OFSTED 4
objectives 6, 16, 23–4, 42, 5
    using ICT to meet 94–1
'Ourselves' topic 55, 58–
'out of step' children 30

outcome, differentiation by 15–16
Oxfordshire: Catch Up programme 4, 20

parent helpers 7, 8
phonics 80
   programmes 20–21
phonological awareness 72
   programmes 20
Phonographix 22
planning
   for behaviour difficulties 36–42
   for complex needs class 57, **63–8**
   differentiated 46–52
   for speech and language impaired children 76, 77
   for vision impaired children 83, 84–5, 86
plenary 3, 8, 12, **17**, 18, **31**, **32**, 35, 36–7, 40, 76, 77, 86, 90
prompts 38

QCA Examplar Scheme of Work for ICT 92, 94–104
questions 10, 47

read and draw/read and do 15
reading 13, **57**
   guided 10–11, 25–6, **32**, 47, **65**, **68**, 75, 79, 80, 84–5, 89–90
   instructional **33**
   shared 10, 17, 18, 75, 77, 82–3, 87–9
Reading Recovery 4, 19
reading schemes 22
reception **94**
reinforcement 26, **28**, **29**
resources **33**
rewards 11, 37, 41
rhyming 26, **29**
ritual 37
routine 37
rules 36–7

SEN 2, 3, 4–6, 7, 8, 9, 10, 12, 15, 18, 27, **28**
seating 9, 46–7, 78
seeing 9
sentence level work 14, 15, 16, 24, **33**, **57**, **72**, 74–5 *see also* word and sentence level work
sequencing 14
setting 5
severe learning difficulties 70
shared reading 10, **17**, 18, 75, 77, 82–3, 87–9 *see also* shared text work
shared text work 3, 8, **31**, **32**, 35, 40, 47, **63**, **66**, 79, 80 *see also* shared reading; shared time; shared writing
shared time 35, **35**, 37, 40, 47 *see also* shared text work; word and sentence level work
shared writing 10, **17**, 18, 77, 83–4, 87–9 *see also* shared text work

sign bilingual learners 80
signals 11, 40–41
skills, behavioural 35, **35**, 36
software 93–4
sorting 14
Sound Beginnings 20
Soundworks 21
Special Educational Needs Coordinator (SENCO) 7
specific learning difficulties 13
speech and language difficulties 70–77
spelling and punctuation software 93
structured programmes 19–22
   developing your own 23–9
support staff 6, 7–8, 86 *see also* adults; Learning Support Assistant
'switch off', problem of 53–4

THRASS 21
talking books software 93
'Talking Computer' programme 21–2
task board 11, 47
task cards/sheets 11, 49
tasks
   types of 13–15
   differentiation of 15–16, 47, 49
team approach 7–9
Teletubbies 54–5
text decoding software 93
text level work 14, 15, 16, 24, **33**, **57**, **72**, 75
text marking 14
transition points 37–8

verbs 16, **16**, **51**, **52**
vision impairment, children with 5, 70, 81–6
vocabulary, difficulty in learning 79

withdrawal 4
word and sentence level work 3, 8, **17**, 18, 26, **28**, **32**, 35, 40, 47, 49, **64**, **67**, 84, 89 *see also* sentence level work; word level work
word level work 5, 10, 14, 15, 16, 24, 26, **28**, **33**, **57**, **72**, 72–4 *see also* word and sentence level work
word lists 6, **6**, 7, **7**
word processors 93
word puzzles 93
writing 13–14, **57**
   guided **65**, **68**, 80, 85, 89–90
   shared 77, 83–4, 87–9

Year 1   **95**
Year 2   34, **96–7**
Year 3   **17**, 20, 22, **98–9**
Year 4   22, 34, **100–101**
Year 5   **102–3**
Year 6   **104**